Communication

The One Stop Series

Series editor: David Martin, FCIS, FIPD, FCB
            Buddenbrook Consultancy

A series of practical, user-friendly yet authoritative titles designed to provide a one stop guide to key topics in business administration.

Other books in the series to date include:

David Martin	*One Stop Company Secretary*
David Martin	*One Stop Personnel*
Jeremy Stranks	*One Stop Health and Safety*
John Wyborn	*One Stop Contracts*
David Martin	*One Stop Property*
Harris Rosenberg	*One Stop Finance*
Robert Leach	*One Stop Payroll*
David Martin/ John Wyborn	*One Stop Negotiation*

1998 Titles

Karen Huntingford	*One Stop Insurance*
Robin Ellison	*One Stop Pensions*
Patrick Forsyth	*One Stop Marketing*
David Martin	*One Stop Customer Care*

ONE STOP
Communication

DAVID MARTIN

ICSA Publishing
The Official Publishing Company of
The Institute of Chartered Secretaries and Administrators

in association with

Prentice Hall Europe

London New York Toronto Sydney Tokyo Singapore
Madrid Mexico City Munich Paris

First published 1998 by
ICSA Publishing Limited
Campus 400, Maylands Avenue
Hemel Hempstead
Hertfordshire, HP2 7EZ

Typeset in 10/12.5 pt Meridien with Frutiger Light
by Hart McLeod, Cambridge

Printed and bound in Great Britain
by MPG Books Ltd, Bodmin, Cornwall

British Library Cataloguing in Publication Data

A catalogue record for this book is available from
the British Library

ISBN: 1-860-72043-9

1 2 3 4 5 02 01 00 99 98

Contents

Preface   vii

Part 1 Skills

Active listening   3

Arrogance   9

Communicating internally   15

Electronic transmissions   23

Graphics and illustrations   31

Jargon   37

Letters, memos, etc.   43

Notice boards   49

Presentations   53

Problem people   59

Report writing   67

Telephoning   73

Temper   79

Video and TV   83

Part 2 Challenges

Aims   89

Annual General Meeting   93

Annual report   99

Bad news   107

Briefing   113

Carelines 119

Communication policy 123

Community relations 127

Conferences (press, sales, etc.) and exhibitions 129

Consultation channels 135

Corporate style 139

Crisis communication 145

Customer care 151

Departmental newsletters 157

Disciplinary interviews 161

Employee reports 165

External actions 171

Handbooks 175

Induction 181

International challenges 187

Interviewing 193

Joint consultation 199

Journals and newsletters 203

Meetings 209

Mentoring 217

Organisation charts 219

Press releases 223

Public relations 227

Suggestion schemes 235

Summary financial statements 239

VIPs 243

Web site and the internet 247

Zygote 251

Preface

Of all business words, 'communication' must be one of those in most common use. This is hardly surprising since communication is crucial to human life and endeavour. Leading firm of consultants McKinsey estimate that by the year 2000, 70% of all European jobs will require professional skills (implying education to A level or above). The Confederation of British Industry, commenting on this research, stated that 'outstanding communication skills' will be needed by these employees.

In reality however the word 'communication' is often misused. People guilty of such misuse include:

- Those who claim 'our communication is excellent' and in evidence produce handbooks, annual reports, procedure manuals, newsletters and so on. Such documentation may be excellent – and essential – but it is not communication.
- Those who state that their internal communication is first class because their chief exccutive regularly makes presentations to the employees. This is admirable and valuable but it is not communication.
- Those who describe the provision of excellent product and service data to their customers as 'first-class communication'. Again the documentation is of real value – but it is not communication.

'We have a communication problem' runs an oft-repeated cry. True – but in reality 'we' have three problems – of definition, of application and of interpretation.

Definition

The definition problem is simply stated, absolutely vital but often entirely overlooked. We tend to use the word 'communication' when actually we mean 'information'.

If A, a manager, tells B, a member of his staff, that there is a requirement for B to produce 1000 widgets by next Friday (or, worse, sends him an e-mail or memo), very often A will regard himself as having communicated with B. In fact this is rubbish – all that has happened is that B is in receipt of some information (which he may or may not understand). If B is in the situation that he has half his team away sick, there is an overtime ban preventing the remaining part of the team from working longer and there is a problem obtaining raw material from stores, there is little possibility of him complying with A's request. However, only if B replies 'no chance' and explains his problems (i.e. provides feedback) does a communicative process start.

Application

As its name implies 'communication' requires a dialogue – a meeting of minds between two or more parties. Where the parties are face to face it is possible that communication will ensue even if it was not intended. If the two are face to face, B's body language, even if he utters no words, may well provide a message to A (provided A is prepared to look for and appreciate such messages). It is said that, when face-to-face, words are only 7% of the message.

However, face-to-face communication, invaluable although it is, is possible in only a minority of the instances when we wish to 'communicate' with our target audience. Or do we wish to communicate at all? Are we not in the position that all we want to do is to inform them? There is nothing wrong with this process – indeed it may be essential and, in some cases, even a legal requirement. The danger comes when we assume that this one-way simple (easy to generate) provision of information is the same as a dynamic, two-way dialogue which is true communication.

Interpretation

Because we learned to talk without formal teaching and others do reply when we use the skill, we tend to assume that we know how to communicate and that others will always understand what we mean. However, research indicates that such an assumption is false.

If we read information (without making notes) on average we will retain around 10% of the subject matter.

If we hear information (with no opportunity to ask questions or take notes) we will retain around 20%.

If we see information (e.g. a video) we will retain about 30%.

If we see and hear information (e.g. at a presentation) we will retain about 50%.

If we are involved in the information provision so that we have an input we will retain about 70%.

If the information is provided in a learning situation (e.g. a trainee talks his/her way through a process) we will retain about 90%.

The golden rule to remember in seeking to start communicating is to frame the data with the interests of the target audience in mind.

Nowadays, in addition to traditional means of conveying information, there is a whole panoply of technological developments – faxes, voice-mail, e-mail, the internet, intranets and so on – that are excellent information transmission tools. Such developments are obviously welcome but we need to guard against assuming that in using them we are communicating – we are not; all we have done is to speed up the transmission and recording of information – nothing more. The barriers to communication set out in the above panel remain.

This book

The subject of this book is communication, but in no way does it communicate. It cannot since I the author cannot obtain feedback (much as I would welcome your guidance) from you the reader. A book can only seek to inform and here we have gathered together a résumé of a range of skills (in Part 1) and descriptions of the methods by which organisations can begin the communication process (in Part 2), in order to make available suggestions of approaches that can be used in the wide variety of situations where those organisations need to inform/communicate with their target audiences – be they employees, shareholders, customers, the media, and so on, and can try to overcome some of the barriers set out above. Perhaps somewhat inevitably there is a bias of content towards the internal challenges, given that the need for communication with employees is constant and continuous. However, if management and employees can communicate effectively inevitably this will lead to more positive communication with and the transmission of clearer messages to the other, external, parties with whom all organisations should seek to communicate. In addition such a process will aid productivity.

Putting the requirement in perspective

As management educator Peter Drucker said recently 'the solutions to organisational problems frequently lie not in the executive suite but in the collective intelligence of the workforce.'

How can we tap that collective intelligence unless we foster real dynamic, two-way communication?

A report (*Impact of People Management Practices on Business Performance* Patterson, West, Lawthom and Nickell, IPD, 1998) concludes 'The results suggest that if managers wish to influence the performance of their companies the most important area they should emphasise is the management of people. This is ironic, given that our research has also demonstrated that emphasis on human resource management is one of the most neglected areas of managerial practice within organisations.'

How can management manage – or, more importantly and effectively, lead – their employees unless they communicate actively with them?

In reviewing worldwide communication research over the last 20 years, Dr Jon White of the City University Business School found a consistent correlation between high business performance and good organisational communication.

How can we seek to convert our target audiences (both internal and external) to our own way of thinking unless we provide clear information, and attempt to start a two-way communication process?

As Franklin D. Roosevelt said 'The art of being a great leader is to get people to do what you want them to do because they want to do it.' If we seek to communicate we seek to lead – if we seek to lead we first need to learn how to communicate effectively.

David M. Martin
Buddenbrook, January 1998

PART 1
Skills

Active listening

Introduction

In October 1997 a report in *The Director* (the monthly journal of the Institute of Directors) it was claimed that one in four workers in Britain feels under-utilised in their job – leaving them bored, stressed and demotivated. Chief Executive of Investors in People, Mary Chapman, was quoted as saying 'Boredom and frustration at work is often the result of an employee's lack of involvement with the company's goals and a feeling that their ideas are not wanted.'

In an earlier survey, MORI found that 33% of employees felt they could do more work without too much effort. This potential went unexploited, however, largely it might be suggested because in the same survey 53% of those asked felt management was more interested in giving its own point of view than in listening to what employees had to say. Another survey by financial recruitment specialists Robert Half discovered that nearly half the managers interviewed did not put aside any time to talk to (let alone listen to) their staff.

Message appreciation

Research indicates that when two parties are face to face, the words they utter comprise only around 7% of the complete message. The overwhelming mass of signals regarding their words (and the meaning the speaker intended to give to those words) which comprise the vast proportion of the total message is derived from

* tone, language, inflexion of the sounds received and
* the manner in which the words are delivered, that is the body language of the speaker (which itself can be affected by the body language of the listener).

Example

If one speaker says to another in a lighthearted tone (for example in response to a none-too-serious insult) 'I am going to kill you', whilst smiling broadly, it is unlikely that the listener will take the words seriously. Conversely if the same listener was confronted alone on a dark night by a masked man wielding a knife saying the same words but in a thoroughly menacing tone, it would be hardly surprising if his comprehension of the words – as well as his reaction – wasn't somewhat different.

The message is simple – yet surprisingly often, and in many walks of life, overlooked. If we are trying to start a communicative process with a target audience (which means that we wish to encourage feedback and response, otherwise we are simply providing information and not attempting to communicate at all) then we need to be prepared to listen to and appreciate the real messages provided by that feedback and response. Words themselves are only a tiny part of the message we need to appreciate.

In fact, even though no thought may have been undertaken in terms of ensuring the recipient could understand the message, when the parties are face to face, the chances of true communication are high. After all, in the example (cited in the Preface) of A requiring B to generate 1000 widgets by Friday, in many situations one could expect B's response (given the circumstances in which he finds himself) to be immediate and robust. With the benefit of that response, the communicative process can begin, and provided A is reasonable, understanding leading to some kind of compromise can be reached. A will in turn need to consider B's response – it may be genuine, but equally B may be trying to manipulate the situation for any number of reasons. A will therefore need to probe B's explanation by questioning and checking – which can occur immediately.

This is, however, only the situation when the two parties are face to face. When the parties are remote and the communication medium is not 'face-to-face verbal' but written (either in hard-copy or by electronic connection) the likelihood of shared understanding is made immeasurably harder. Tone, inflexion, facial expression and other body language are lost and all that replaces them are words which can mean very different things to different people.

Example

'Causal' has an entirely different meaning to 'casual' and yet the person reading at speed the sentence 'it is suggested that there is a causal link between the procedure and the accident...'

as

'it is suggested that there is a casual link between the procedure and the accident...'

will gain a vastly different impression to that intended. Presumably the writer meant to imply that the procedure needed to be changed to prevent another accident – an inference not remotely suggested by the second version.

Similarly,

'I think we now agree that the businesses are not complementary.'

takes on an entirely new meaning if the reader reads or receives it as

'I think we now agree that the businesses are not complimentary'.

In both these instances it could have been the typist who misunderstood the words (itself an important link often overlooked in the consideration of the framing of the message required to pass between originator and reader). This is a timely reminder that written items need to be checked carefully by the originator if they are not to be a causal link of poor communication and, in the process, a not particularly complimentary reflection on the author (who failed to check the typing)!

Case study: How interesting

In a dispute which had led to a tribunal hearing the employers received a letter from their former employee's representative stating 'unless you are able to collect these items by 31st March this will be impossible until October, as the house is being sold and all Mrs Bloggs's goods and shackles are being placed in storage for six months'.

Presumably the would-be communicator (actually the ex-employee's husband) meant to have said 'goods and chattels' which is a term possibly appropriate in a legal document but hardly in this kind of letter. However, the fact that the inappropriate JARGON was misheard and typed as 'shackles' provided illumination on the kind of person the writer was (careless enough not to check his correspondence before signing it) – or else providing a fascinating insight to their relationship!

Constructing the right message

Before any consideration of the feedback (which is essential before communication can commence) we need to ensure that the message we intend to deliver is absolutely correct. 'Correct' in this context means that it reflects what we really wish to say, that the language and words used are correct, and that our message is couched in language and format appropriate to (i.e. 'can be clearly understood by') the target audience. It also needs to be such that it does not reflect poorly on the writer – the reputation of the writer in the above case study was hardly enhanced by the mistaken word, whilst the reputation of neither writer nor organisation was enhanced by the letter featured in ARROGANCE.

The need to provide the right message can be encapsulated in the prime guidance to all who seek to communicate (which basically means every person on Earth).

If the reader or listener does not understand the message as was intended – the responsibility is that of the writer or speaker.

The obvious truth of this statement (again in practice often overlooked) is that the whole reason for writing or speaking should be so that the receiver can understand what the sender wishes to say. Sadly, it seems that in a number of instances the writer or speaker thinks only in terms of what he or she wishes to say and the interests of the recipient are subordinated to that preference.

Indeed, in some cases, a person will speak or write apparently only with the aim of bolstering their own ego or to attempt to increase their own reputation in the eyes of the recipient (see examples quoted in JARGON). Whilst this may be an understandable ploy, in no way does it approach a genuine basis for communication – and neither is it likely to generate genuine feedback or response. In such a case no matter how great the commitment to active listening, the true message is unlikely to 'get through'.

The effect

The danger of not constructing the right message, or of constructing the right message but then not transmitting it accurately, or of constructing and transmitting it accurately but then not listening actively to the response, is that we can be trapped into assuming that we understand what our target audience are thinking or saying which in turn can lead us into misconceptions and false assumptions. In some instances this process is totally ignored and an arrogant assumption is made that the originator knows and understands what the target audience views are or what their response will be. Whilst on occasion a correct assumption will be made, it is a high-risk policy, basically since any organisation or originator which does not listen to the views of their target audience can be trapped into making incorrect decisions, thereby alienating them.

Case study: Unelected

The scale of the defeat of the Conservative Party in the General Election of 1997 surprised many people. Yet this should not have been the case since the view was widespread amongst its own supporters that those in charge of the party were either not reflecting or not listening to (or both) the views of those supporters at voter level. Over a number of years of local elections the Party's 'grass-roots' support had been whittled away and it seemed that little attention was being paid to trying to restore these foundations. If people are ignored or their views not taken into account it is hardly surprising if they withdraw support. (In that instance their plight was exacerbated by the fact that their opponents were listening very carefully and apparently responding in terms of policy commitment to the wishes expressed by those whose views they sought.)

Checklist: Key techniques

1. Identify the target audience.
2. Identify the message to be transmitted and the information to be sought in return.
3. Generate accurate information using language which is clear, concise and understandable.
4. Identify an appropriate mode to transmit the information to the target audience and by which feedback can be obtained.
5. Transmit the information (indicating the manner in which feedback can be transmitted in turn).
6. Listen to and consider the feedback.
7. Consider the next step. This could mean action, but equally it could require further communication to identify additional information, answers to further questions, and so on.
8. Don't assume anything. Remember the adage 'never assume – it makes an ASS of U and ME'. Over 80% of assumptions turn out to be false.
9. Respond accordingly.
10. Above all, construct simple clear messages.

Arrogance

Introduction

To engender communication takes confidence – either confidence that the reputation of the initiator and/or organisation will be enhanced as a result, or that both will have the ability to react where criticism is generated by the process. In most instances, understandably the accent is on the positive. However, in a number of the sections in this book, warnings and notes are included, since the dividing line between confidence in what one is doing and arrogance in believing without question that one has all the right answers can be very fine. The aim of this section is to sound a note of caution for the ears of the communicator, since it is all too easy to overstep the 'confidence line' and to descend into arrogance.

Aims

In many ways the guidance to the manner and format of items to be communicated and discussed will be found in the AIMS adopted by the organisation, since these act as a criteria as much in terms of approach as in content. It is extremely unlikely that such aims will include a warning against arrogance, although confidence and success which are most organisations' understandable aims can be a breeding ground for over-confidence – potentially as dangerous as a lack of confidence. Sadly there are numerous examples of both executives and organisations becoming so confident and self-assured that they come to believe that they and their organisation can do no wrong. Very often this attitude at the top of an organisation conceals the fact that lower down there are severe problems, and that amongst their customers is an irritation that such problems, many of which may be fundamental, are ignored by those ultimately responsible. The Chinese have a saying that 'the fish rots from the head'. If there are problems in an organisation – the responsibility for dealing with them rests with those at the top, and only those at the top can correct them. Moreover, they can only correct them if they know what is going on throughout the organisation.

Sharp-end analysis

To ensure that complacency (the breeding ground for arrogance) does not become endemic, top management need to appreciate that in addition to it being their responsibility to take decisions and bring about actions to meet targets and criteria, it is also their responsibility to ensure this is carried out **in the way they wanted it**. Too often authority is not so much delegated as abdicated, leading to a situation where those with an imperfect knowledge or understanding of what is required take decisions or generate attitudes at variance to those required by the Board. There needs to be adequate (if tactful) policing and checking at the levels between those that make decisions and those that carry them out, to ensure that the messages are actually being interpreted in the way intended.

Case study: That's not what I meant

Number One felt that the organisation needed a boost to its morale and addressed all the senior managers, stressing the fact that there were new orders to be won which would ensure the factories worked to capacity for at least a year. One of the aims of the address was to reassure everyone that there was no question of short-time working or losing reliable employees through redundancy. The request was to pass the message on 'right through the whole company'.

The senior managers went away and saw the middle and junior managers. The message the latter heard, however, was 'we've got an awful lot to do in the next year, so get everyone cracking on it – only the reliable are safe'.

In turn the junior managers saw their supervisors and passed them the message that 'we really need to crack down on everything for the next 12 months'.

The supervisors, some of whom were having discipline problems, saw this as an opportunity and told their employees, 'unless you lot pull your fingers out and improve productivity you'll all be out of jobs by the end of the year'.

The trade union representatives were extremely concerned that redundancies might be in the offing and immediately requested a meeting with the Chief Executive at which they threatened a work-to-rule unless the full facts were put before them.

Key point: Making oneself understood can be difficult at the best of times but when one's message needs to be passed through several intermediaries, almost inevitably it will be misinterpreted, misconstrued and misunderstood.

It is generally accepted that each time a message is passed on, between 15% and 25% of the meaning will be lost – and that assumes the parties genuinely wished to pass on the message. In some cases those involved may deliberately distort or suppress part or all of the message.

Sharp-end effect

If the requirements are not being adhered to there is a danger that what is actually happening, and seen to be happening by the people that matter (e.g. the customers) is not what was required by the Board. If corporate pronouncements are then made which trumpet the Board's policy, which are manifestly not in tune with the experience of the customer, the credibility of the Board (and indeed of the whole organisation) is inevitably suspect – and, figuratively speaking, there could well be a considerable smell of rotting fish! Board members themselves need to know from personal investigation that what is stated to be 'policy' is actually being carried out in 'practice'. Equally they cannot afford to rely on messages being conveyed to them by intermediaries. For a number of reasons these may be distorted or filtered (see BRIEFING) either in dissemination or in feedback (or both).

Case study: Pointless

A monopolistic landlord had a large number of outlets leased or let to a range of businesses and individuals. One long-term lessee was somewhat bemused and not a little irritated to receive the following letter:

Covenant enforcement
You have been found to be in breach of the terms of the Tenancy Agreement. Please remove all stickers/posters displayed on the windows/doors and unit front. The unit should then be redecorated in appropriate colours where necessary. Retail goods on display should be well presented and the area kept clean and tidy at all times.
    I hereby give you four weeks in which to comply with this Notice. Otherwise I will have no alternative but to take further action on this matter.

The lessee had previously enjoyed a good working arrangement with the landlord, paying the rent on time, etc., and could have been excused for responding robustly to both the content and the tone of this ill-thought-out missive. Firstly there is a difference between a 'tenancy agreement' and the lease which was in operation here. Secondly although the lease contained various covenants there was no prohibition on the display of posters in the windows. Thirdly the responsibility for the tidiness of the shop was that of the lessee and it was kept tidy – whereas the area outside the shop (the responsibility of the landlord) was often untidy.

When the lessee challenged the letter he was told that

- it was a 'standard letter' to all holders of tenancy agreements (not the case here)

- it referred to cases where posters, etc., had been attached to the exterior of premises (not the case here)

- it was a written confirmation of previously made verbal comments (not the case here)

- the redecoration referred to the possibility that in removing exterior posters, paintwork could be damaged and should be repaired (which is hardly clear from the wording used which refers to the 'unit' being 'redecorated').

Corporate arrogance here allowed the conceit that one standard letter, written in a brusque, even offensive, style could cover a multitude of different cases. Here it served only to irritate a responsible lessee and to reflect poorly on the organisation that could allow such an ill-conceived communication to be sent.

Seeing it as it is

At all times the reality of the situation needs to be borne in mind. Normally what sells well today is actually yesterday's product or service (that is it was developed yesterday and is being fully exploited now). The challenge for today is to develop tomorrow's product. This could be a derivative of yesterday's product, but is more likely (if it is to be really successful in a fast moving and changing world of demand) to be something different. A failure to appreciate that demand and reputation can be fickle friends has been the death of many organisations. The only way to combat this complacency is to communicate with the market and those assessing and projecting the market (i.e. actively seek objective feedback) – and to be prepared to accept criticism rather than simply dismissing it as 'ill-informed' or 'imperfectly based'. Those best placed to communicate with the market are employees at the sharp end, but the Board needs to ensure they have been properly briefed and fully understand its aims, policies and attitudes.

Markets – by which here we mean consumers – have a habit of showing the organisation that thinks it knows it all, that in fact it had imperfect perception. Reputations (and demand) can take years to create and seconds to lose. The use of CARELINES, CUSTOMER CARE and market research not just on the products but also on the perception of the organisation can be valuable. Possibly the most useful advice is to quote Oliver Cromwell: 'I beseech you, in the bowels of Christ, think it possible you may be mistaken' – and to take action accordingly.

Thinking it possible that we might be wrong does not mean lacking confidence in what we are doing; it is merely a warning that we should always be checking to ensure we have got it right – not least since the situation in which we find ourselves is always fluid. Nowhere is this more necessary than in communication. Because we have promulgated a message we can assume neither that the message has reached the correct target, nor that the target has understood it; nor even that if it has been received and understood in the way that we intended. As my first boss used to say 'Don't assume, Martin – find out'. The tone and words might have belonged to a different age of employee relations – the value of the advice lives on. Organisations and communicators cannot afford to assume – that is corporate and managerial arrogance – we all need to find out all the time.

Communicating internally

Introduction

Organisations have only two tangible assets – money (the value or 'conversion' of which may appear in various forms) and people. Thriving and expanding businesses depend largely on the exploitation of ideas by the successful manipulation of the money and the ongoing and successful motivation of the people. Employees are often described as the greatest assets of the organisation, and indeed without their effort and work nothing can be achieved. As Sir John Harvey Jones comments in *Making it Happen* (Collins, 1988): **'with the best will in the world and the best board in the world, and the best strategic direction in the world, nothing will happen unless everyone down the line understands what they are trying to achieve and gives of their best'.**

Good-quality, trained and committed employees can improve the perception and performance of the organisation as much as poor-quality and poorly motivated employees can mar and blunt it. Whilst it is important to communicate externally it is absolutely vital to communicate internally, since unless employees understand

- what their employer is trying to do

- how their efforts and jobs contribute to the business and how they can help, and

- how and why decisions need to be made, and made the way they are,

there may not be material, products or services (of the required quality) to be communicated about externally. As Jeffrey Pfeffer of the Harvard Business School stated: 'What successful firms tend to have in common is that for their sustained advantage, they rely not on technology, patents or strategic position, but on how they manage their people'. Indeed it is only through people that technology, patents or strategy can be developed and exploited.

Value

The Advisory, Conciliation and Arbitration Service (ACAS) has for over 20 years been involved in the process of trying to improve relationships in the workplace. In 1994 ACAS published a guide *Employee Communications and Consultation* noting that during the 1980s and 1990s it had seen an increasing emphasis on regarding employees as 'human resources', whose abilities could be improved (even exploited) in order to increase productivity. According to ACAS 'good' employee communication has a 'measurable effect on organisational success' through improved management decision-making, greater trust and increased job satisfaction. The report defines employee communications as

> the provision and EXCHANGE [author's capitals] of information and instructions which enable an organisation to function efficiently,

and states that communication is an integral part of every manager's job. The report goes on to suggest ways in which the process can be effected.

Checklist: Internal communication process

1. A clear statement of policy should be drawn up (see COMMUNICATION POLICY).
2. Those responsible at each level should be identified (see ORGANISATION CHARTS).
3. The means by which communication is promulgated and encouraged should be established (via a procedure possibly repeated as part of the policy).
4. Those responsible for the communication process, as well as those with whom the organisation wishes to communicate, should be trained.
5. The whole system should be monitored regularly.

The extension of employee share ownership which inevitably requires additional company–employee communication tends to generate improved performance. A report by Capital Strategies in 1997 (*Financial Times (FT)* report, 28 April 1997) indicated that between 1992 and 1996, 30 companies which had 10% or more of their shares held by employees other than directors had outperformed the FTSE All Share Index by 89%. In the USA the American sister organisation of Capital Strategies reported that between 1992 and 1995 public companies with more than 10% employee share ownership had generated a return of over 80%, whereas the return for all companies on the Dow Jones index for the same period was only 49%.

Case study: Putting it into perspective

During the Second World War, King George VI attempted to aid civilian morale by many personal visits. On visiting an engineering works he found employees in good heart although apparently unaware of the importance of the locking nuts they were producing. In fact the nuts were used as part of the fastening of propellers to the Spitfire – the aircraft critical to the winning of the Battle of Britain – that the country was desperately trying to produce. When the King discovered their ignorance, he insisted that the staff were told. It is said that output increased considerably because the employees then understood the vital importance of their task.

> **Key technique**
>
> Basically people cannot care about something that they do not know or understand. The more people care, the more committed they can become to the aims of the endeavour. Perhaps communication could be defined as a process that helps people understand and CARE in order to tie their efforts closely to the ultimate aims.

Defining the requirement

Whilst examples of the instances which require a communicative process are set out in COMMUNICATION POLICY, the means by which these instances can be achieved need to be considered.

Checklist: Initial communication considerations

1. *What is the purpose of this communicative process?*
   Very often we start to inform third parties (deluding ourselves that we are communicating when we are not – or at least not yet) without a clear vision of what it is we are trying to achieve. Unless we define our 'desired result' on each occasion, our effort at communication may be doomed from the start. Further we may need to consider whether what we are undertaking is actually a process of negotiation – if it is then we should approach the whole interface as negotiation using a process of communication. (See David Martin and John Wyborn, *One Stop Negotiation,* ICSA Publishing/Prentice Hall, 1997.)

2. *What is my target audience?*
   Defining the target audience and their interests and requirements may help define the desired result – and vice versa.
3. *Are they likely to be interested automatically or will I need to work hard to capture their attention?*
   The words 'work hard' were a deliberate choice here (as most phrases in any communicative work should be) to emphasise that the onus is on the initiator to gain and retain the attention of the target and to encourage their reaction. This may require a considerable amount of attention – communication takes time. Unfortunately it seems that too often messages are constructed with too little consideration for the words used – and their meaning to others – and even the effect on them.

Case study: Paid off

It seems in some cases that the only time an employer really talks to his employees is when he is about to dispense with them. However, even when this occurs some take the opportunity to confuse and irritate rather than explain and elucidate.

> As a result of this downsizing, there will be surplus productive capacity and the employer proposes for those affected a not ungenerous compensation package.

Research indicates that, to employees, 'downsizing' is one of the most hated words. This is possibly not so much for what the word implies (i.e. redundancies) as for the pompous arrogance of using jargon to try to hide BAD NEWS. If the news was not bad enough, its effect is worsened by the user of such words patronising his audience – and leaving them in limbo since they have no idea when the next stage occurs. Further, one word which may jump off the page and hit those in receipt of such a memo is 'ungenerous'. The immediate reaction may be (since many may well skim rather than study the memo) 'not only are they getting rid of us, they are not going to be generous'. Finally, whether the package is 'not ungenerous' or 'generous' may depend whether you are giving or receiving.

You only have one chance to make a first impression and the writer might have been well advised to have stated:

'Unfortunately the organisation will need to declare some employees redundant. A compensation package is being arranged. Details will be discussed individually on [date].'

---

4. *How will this target audience best be able to receive the message I have to give, and how can I best generate a situation through which the other party can respond?*

    Often what the initiator generates is information in the form that readily springs to their mind. However, this is seeing the subject matter through the wrong eyes. We need to see the message through the eyes of the target audience. If the recipient does not understand the message the responsibility is that of the initiator.

5. *What is the best medium to use?*

    The most effective way of achieving communication may be by using the human voice and face. Although circumstances where the two parties are literally in one place may be difficult to achieve, video links, telephone conferencing and even audio cassette programmes could be used as a substitute. With interactive video and TV links (and to a lesser extent the telephone conferencing links) live voice and facial contact can be gained. Using audio cassettes (which can be reproduced in large numbers relatively cheaply) can gain the advantage of the listener being able to hear the message with emphasis and expression otherwise entirely lacking from written material.

6. *What is the best language to use?* (see JARGON)

    Our language (that is the words we may use naturally) may not be the language used by the target audience. MORI found in surveys that 'process re-engineering', 'delayering' and 'downsizing' are not generally understood and thus disliked by employees ('empowerment', 'delighting the customer', 'culture change' and 'mission statement' are also disliked). If we insist on using jargon and disliked words, we will create barriers between ourselves and our target audience – hardly the best foundation on which to try to build a communicative process.

7. *What is the best written means to use?*

    Unfortunately the composition of LETTERS, memos, NOTICES, etc., is not always given the attention it requires and false or misleading messages are sometimes conveyed. The perhaps inevitable result is that misunderstandings result and communication is not achieved. We need to recognise the limitations of the written process – every word and phrase we use should be weighed carefully to ensure it conveys our intent in the best way possible. Readers cannot ask a question of a piece of paper – or rather they cannot gain an answer from it. When they read, there may be no one available to provide clarification or explanation. If there are unanswered questions, there can be no real communication.

8. *Having prepared the item* – ask someone not involved to assess the message trying to be achieved and only use it if the assessment is in accord with the intent.

19

SARAH

Although it is probably true that the best communicators and leaders are born, all of us can practise to improve. The principles of good direct communication and discussion can be summed up in the process described by the mnemonic SARAH. Although SARAH was originated for use more in selling, her principles apply equally to all one-to-one relationships.

Checklist: SARAH

Smile and stop talking: The emphasis is on letting the other person do the talking (as the Greek philosopher Zeto of Citium said 'the reason we have one mouth and two ears is that we may listen the more and talk the less'), for if one's attitude is pleasant and helpful most people are likely to respond. But then we need to be prepared to listen. This may mean trying to discover attitudes and opinions in advance – easy to achieve when face to face, but essential whatever method of communication is being used. Smiling (even when using the phone) relaxes the vocal cords and indicates to the other party a relaxed attitude to which many respond accordingly. Thus it helps to build a rapport. (In Japan some of those who use the phone bow to one another as if they are meeting.)

Case study: Using laughter

The use of laughter is underrated. In the nursery a baby laughs around 450 times a day – sadly the average adult laughs only around 15 times a day, often because tradition suggests that certain things need to be taken with a degree of seriousness. Whilst not suggesting we should trivialise matters, regarding everything as unnecessarily serious may actually help no-one. The responses of many delegates on the 50 or so seminars the author gives each year suggest that most people prefer a little lightheartedness and controlled humour to leaven the working day – and contribute more if it is present.

Active Listening: the corollary to ceasing to hammer home one's point of view to the exclusion of that of the listener is to listen more. Hearing is purely a mechanical act, whereas listening entails active consideration of both what is said and what is left unsaid. Only if we listen to both 'messages' are we likely to gain the real views of the other party. The longer people talk the more they reveal of their true feelings – this may mean that conversations must last longer – but this should result in better understanding leading to improved commitment.

Repetition of content: to show that the other party has understood exactly what was said or written, key sentences or comments could be repeated in different words and the other party asked to confirm that the 'translation' is correct. This has four advantages:

- it helps fix details of the matter in the mind
- it helps check that what has been received was what was meant
- it engenders a rapport and understanding between the two parties, and
- it leads to accurate comprehension of the points made by both parties.

Act with empathy: this entails showing the other party that their views, opinions and motivation are understood. This is true no matter what the circumstances and requires the would-be communicator to have some perception of the interests and requirements of the other party.

Handle the subject matter with appreciation of the feelings of the other party which of course can only be achieved if the communicator tries to place themselves in the position of the other party. This is particularly true when BAD NEWS needs to be communicated.

Electronic transmissions

Introduction

Having for over one hundred years enjoyed a postal service which could deliver (albeit at times imperfectly) written evidence of our thoughts within a matter of days, and for around 60 years enjoyed a telephone service which progressively reduced this transmission period to minutes or seconds, but only in verbal form, we now have available e-mail, intranets and the internet which can deliver our thoughts instantly (like the phone) but with the benefit of the recipient being able to obtain a hard copy for their records (like the post). In theory this should mean that communication should improve. In fact, there is a possibility that despite the marvels of technology, unless we use the process wisely and with adequate thought, communication can actually be impaired, even though the process of the actual dissemination of information is far faster. The problem is related not to electronics but to our assessment of and reaction to the messages being received. Faster and faster transmission is of dubious value if feedback is not engendered and a dialogue encouraged. In ancient times those who brought bad news often suffered personally for their tidings. The instant response of the recipient was to lash out and punish – even execute – someone, usually the unfortunate messenger. Technology gives us the chance to make an instant response – but we need to ask ourselves whether our instant responses are always the best responses.

E-mail

The principle of 'e-mail' is very simple. Using the computer on my desk I am able to link to the computer on my colleague's desk whether we both work for the same organisation (using an intranet) or different organisations (using the internet). Obviously this has great advantages. Unfortunately it also has a considerable number of disadvantages – although at least we will be able to re-read our tele-messages and do not have to rely on our memory of a phone call. Being constantly 'open for business', the memory of one's computer is available to all and sundry to leave messages. Unfortunately, in the same way that the recipient is unable,

23

without switching off the machine, to stop anyone with access to a fax machine wasting his fax paper sending messages, some of which are of little or no value, e-mails, some of which may be of similar worth, can accumulate. Indeed, so great has this problem become that one American legal firm calculated that they were losing a vast amount of their partners' time simply reading non-essential or unsolicited messages (known as 'spam'), and accordingly banned the use of the e-mail system.

Conversely some organisations regard e-mail as being of such priority that all else should be postponed whilst it is dealt with. Some organisations even arrange their system so that use of the computer is only possible once accumulated e-mails have been dealt with. Further action (or at the very least, acknowledgement) is expected virtually immediately. Internally this can aid the free flow of information although the very informality of message and response can lead to problems (see below). However, in an average-sized organisation with everyone enjoying access to an intranet or e-mail system this could mean that each person could have several dozen messages to deal with, ranging from the important to the irrelevant, from those that are essential to the continuation of the business to those that may have been sent more to justify the existence of the sender than for any other (and real) purpose ('ego-mail') – and even to those that harass or bully the recipient ('flame-mail'). The effect is that the recipient has no control over their own priorities. Further the very mass of messages in random order means that valuable time may be wasted dealing with the trivia whilst a vital and urgent message lies buried. Action on such a message may thus be delayed or, should the message itself be overlooked, even ignored.

The permanence of print

In some respects the 'advantage' of the telephone conversation – was the difficulty of retaining an accurate recall of what transpired. American research indicates that only around 11% of the average phone call may be recalled with accuracy. Hence one party can attempt to deny what the other party states was said, and this of course is true of conversation. However, print (including e-mail since the recipient has the capacity to print the messages, or if sent via the Internet to obtain a hard copy for up to two years) has a permanence. Drafting written material tends to involve more time than conversation – even the attention of an extra person (e.g. a typist) provides time for second thoughts. E-mail, however, may lack this time and thought formality, and allows computer users to generate their own messages instantly with the informality of the system encouraging overlooking that first thoughts may be ill-considered. The danger of dealing immediately with items – particularly when faced with a wad of e-mails – is that insufficient 'thought time' is given and thus imperfect thoughts are transmitted once the send key is pressed. This has led some organisations and employees into situations where substantial sums have been awarded against them for libellous remarks made by them using the e-mail system. Currently new law dealing with this situation is awaited – regardless of this care needs to be taken.

Lacking tone

An advantage of the telephone is that, whilst it is not face-to-face communication, nevertheless some body language (if only tone, emphasis and voice sound – some claim to be able to tell when a person is smiling on the phone from their voice sound) can be transmitted and any imperfect understanding can be questioned instantly. When using written language one has the problems that words do not mean the same thing to different people and all words lack tone which can correct such imperfect interpretations of the meaning. The scenario where using e-mail, A misunderstands what B means and responds virtually without thinking in a brusque way, and B, annoyed by what he regards as an irrational and unacceptable answer, responds accordingly and a confrontation is generated is increasingly common. The danger of using an intranet in this way is similar to the old 'memo war' where employees whose offices were only a few yards apart could create antipathy by the use of memos where agreement could have been reached amicably if only one had visited the other's office. In ancient times the Medes and Persians had a rule that one had to make a decision twice – once when drunk and once when sober. At least the passing of the sobering up period provided the opportunity of second thoughts on what would otherwise have been an instant (and perhaps unfortunate) response.

Flame-mail

Electronic confrontation as outlined above may be considered accidental, but unfortunately some use the e-mail system as a weapon either to impose their will or anger on others or as a means of harassing them. In a 1997 survey software producer Novell found that over 500 of a 1000-person sample stated they had received abusive e-mail messages (flame-mail). Further, the evidence showed that about a third of those targeted by flame-mail were equally vitriolic in their response, even though they admitted to finding their productivity substantially impaired for the rest of the day after receipt of a flame-mail.

The simple act of requiring a memo or letter to be typed or word-processed, read and signed and sent, allows several opportunities for second (and subsequent) thoughts. Had the parties been face to face in most cases far more tactful wording (perhaps supported by appropriate facial expressions) would probably have been employed to try to make the point. E-mail has also been used to administer discipline – e.g. sending a warning. Unless this system is referred to within an employer's disciplinary procedure it is likely that it would not be accepted as legitimate, thus leading to potential unfair dismissals; in any event it is unlikely to generate a positive response.

In some organisations, users record and transmit jokes via the e-mail system as they would if meeting by the coffee machine. Many jokes within an organisation tend to revolve around the personalities in that organisation. Whilst it can be argued that whether verbal or written such jokes can add to an informal working atmosphere, there can also be very serious consequences should the wrong person read a message or quip – particularly if it was dashed off with little thought.

Meet the smilies

As referred to earlier when face to face words may account for as little as 7% of the message. The remaining 93% is conveyed by body language, tone, delivery, choice of words, etc. When criticising, complaining or chastising much of the effect of the words can be softened by a smile. Indeed making the point in this way sometimes may be more effective than aggression. This is not possible in written communication and electronic transmission (which tends to lead to abbreviated – and sometime ill-thought-out – sentences) may generate antipathy or even hostility even where no criticism was intended.

These can be offset to a limited extent by using a new language – the 'smilies'. Communication via e-mail is essentially based around the traditional typewriter keyboard, but using the 100 or so characters and letters available there has been created a number of tiny cartoon-like forms which many devotees of e-mail now incorporate into their messages. It could be argued that they are the equivalent of some of the body language that both phone and e-mail lack.

Note: The book must be turned through 90^0 to see the effect.

:-)   The original 'smiley' used to indicate a joke or pleasantry or that the words are not meant to be taken too literally

.-)   The winkie – indicating that it's an aside, again not to be taken too literally

:-(Sad or unhappy

:-II Signifies anger (an emotion which is one of the easiest to indicate in writing – hence the growth of flame-mail)

:-#   Kiss

:-?   I am smoking. . . a pipe

:-i   . . . or a cigarette

:-'   I have a cold

:''-(I'm in tears

:^)   That's put his/her nose out of joint

(:-) Bald-headed

:-0   Yawn yawn

:-/   Undecided

:-1 :-1 Two-faced

:-Y   Speaks with forked tongue

:-x   Keep your mouth shut

(From David Martin, *Tough Telephoning*, Pitman, 1996.)

There are rumoured to be in excess of 600 of these symbols, which, as they come more into common usage, may be capable of providing a little of the facial expression that the reader could have appreciated had they and the writer been face to face. Anything which improves the opportunity for genuine communication is worth trying, and indeed it is not impossible to visualise an e-mail language developing which as a matter of course includes such symbols as well as traditional words.

Usage and control

There is no doubt, particularly in an organisation with remote units or offices, that the advantages of an e-mail system for transmitting information are considerable. Daily updates of information (for example enabling stock-controllers to instruct those in control of the units to change the prices of goods) mean that instant reactions to changing market conditions can be effected. However, the speed of the message should not be allowed to act as a goad to the speed of a considered reply. Instant reactions are not necessarily the best reactions. Accordingly it may be advisable for organisations to publish guidelines for the use of the system.

Example: Intranet (e-mail) procedure

1. E-mail should be used primarily to distribute/update information, confirm arrangements, confirm meetings, etc.

2. As an exception it can be used to leave messages where the recipient is not available and the message can await their return.

3. E-mail should not be used as substitution for face-to-face or telephone conversation.

4. E-mail information is not a substitute for managerial control and should not be used as such.

5. On no account should the system be used for vindictive, harassing, discriminatory or abusive comment or criticism of anyone, whether the target, another employee or any third party.

6. Any person in receipt of an item which they feel should have been prohibited by Note 5 above should produce the item to [name].

7. Any person proved to have deliberately sent an item prohibited by Note 5 above will be deemed guilty of gross misconduct and will be dealt with under the disciplinary procedure accordingly.

8. All messages, etc., should be clear and unambiguous and coded from 5 star to 0 star in order of priority. Clarity is preferable to brevity.

9. An e-mail message should be treated as if it were a hard-copy LETTER and drafted and checked in the same way.

10. No response to an e-mail message should be sent in haste, anger or hostility.

Note: *When using electronic transmission for sending letters, orders, invoices, etc., to third parties, companies should ensure that the document complies with the requirements of the Companies Act and bears the company's registered name, office and number and the country of registration.*

Although it can be difficult to imply a binding contract from a telephone call, if e-mail is used in the same way as a telephone call, a binding contract could be inferred. It may be advisable to require all external correspondence to carry a disclaimer to attempt to indemnify the sponsoring company against improper use of electronic messages or to stipulate that a contractual relationship will only exist when confirmed in hard-copy.

Graphics and illustrations

Introduction

We live in a visually orientated society. Government research in 1997 indicated that the average adult spends the equivalent of 56 days out of every 365 days in a year watching television. Conversely women spend an average of only five days (men, four and a half days) reading each year. General information is more likely to be successfully obtained (ten times more likely based on the above figures) visually than via the written word. In addition this all-pervading use of a visually orientated medium to disseminate information is having an increasing effect on the way written information is presented. Many recipients will accept information far more readily if it is presented in a visually attractive manner. Conversely, the presentation of pages heavy with text, unbroken by any headlines or attention 'grabbers' is unlikely to attract. Hence the use of graphics (in the widest sense of the word) should be considered in presenting information both internally and externally.

Using the medium

The means of generating information are so varied and the weight of information so great that recipients must filter what they receive. Thus to gain the attention of the prospective reader there can be a struggle between competing items. The items that tend to gain attention are those that are user-friendly and require less effort to appreciate. The adage 'a picture is worth a thousand words' is very appropriate in considering communication means. Illustrations in the widest sense of the word are one way of both gaining attention and disseminating some of the content. However, since illustrations tend to provide powerful images they should be used with control – as suggested by the guidelines in the following checklist.

Checklist: Effective page presentation

1. In preparing written material the need to provide a visually stimulating layout, using headlines, subheadings, bold text and illustrations should

be considered. A page should be received as a single composite picture which is how the reader's mind's eye will first perceive it.

2. Illustrations should arise naturally from the text. If this is not possible an explanation for the inclusion of the illustration should be provided. However, to some extent if the illustration needs explanation (other than a simple caption – see 3) it could be argued that it is not performing its task.

3. Photographs and illustrations should be captioned unless they are adequately referred to in immediately adjacent text.

4. In EMPLOYEE REPORTS ideally both products and personnel should be featured – and both should be named. Using photographs of named personnel adds life to the document and rapport between those who helped created the results and the document. Using illustrations of the products helps place the whole document in perspective. If such photographs can also incorporate customers (where applicable) the interests of most of those involved have been reflected.

5. Graphical representations of figures should be simple and two-dimensional. Care must be taken with the use of three-dimensional illustrations because the addition of the relief can suggest a misleading relationship of size.

6. Proportions and scales must be accurate. The eye tends to look at an illustration as a whole and a word as an entity, therefore the 'whole illustration' (not just a detail) must give a true impression. Equally all data must be accurate.

7. In displaying graphs, the use of a 'suppressed zero' should be avoided. A 'suppressed zero' occurs when the base for a graph is not zero but some higher figure. The effect is to overemphasise movements and trends in the graph which, to the unwary or untrained, can give a misleading impression. If, for reasons of space, a suppressed zero must be used, a jagged 'lightning mark' should be used near the base of the vertical axis of the chart to draw attention to the fact that the base is not zero.

8. Percentages are generally not understood – 47% of the UK population have difficulty understanding them. With an audience which might have such difficulty both figures which support the percentage change should be featured.

9. Cartoons and humour can sometimes be used to good effect. However, their use must be controlled and appropriate to the subject matter to avoid trivialising it.

10. All illustrations should be of a decent size. If the reader has to strain to see the illustration it is unlikely that their attention will be retained for long.

11. Colour is a very powerful indicator. If colour-coding items, extreme care must be taken to ensure the two or more disparate items do not share the same or a similar colour.
12. The number of illustrations should be controlled since too many illustrations can be as off-putting as too many words.
13. The text also needs to be regarded as if it were an 'illustration' in its own right. As such, the use of short paragraphs, suitably captioned where necessary or using key words or bold type to guide the reader through the text, can aid the attention of the reader since the impression will be given of a page that contains 'digestible chunks' of information.

See NOTICES and JARGON for further guidance.

The page as illustration

The first and last items in the above checklist both refer to the page itself being an illustration. When confronted by a printed page our mind's eye tends to see the whole as a picture. Most people confronted by a complete page of text will regard it as an immediate 'turn off' – that is they may be repelled from reading further. If, however, this initial picture attracts rather than repels their attention they may well decide to read both that and the following page. Where pages are printed on both sides, when turning the right-hand pages the reader's mind's eye initially sees the resulting double page as a single picture before coming to rest about a third of the way down the right-hand side. Placing a message or illustration in this position may give this item a considerable presence on the page.

Generally most casual readers will prefer to see the information provided on the page in a way that they will find easy to assimilate. This means that paragraphs should be short, headings and subheadings should be used and lines should not break the 2.5 alphabet (i.e. 'not more than 65 characters on a line') rule. If written information is presented in this way (the white space and headings counting for this purpose as 'illustrations') the page of print will have several 'signposts'. The signposts on the pages have two purposes:

1. They point the reader towards the items they are likely to find of interest.
2. They ensure the text does not appear too heavy, which should entice and retain attention, turning the browser into a reader. In the following two illustrations the same piece of text appears. However, in the first

version little thought was given to the interests of the reader. The lines are far too long, the type is too small and there is no guidance for the reader on what to look at. In the second version the double-column layout means a much shorter line and additional amounts of white paper relieve the eye. Headings and subheadings have been used to point the readers to the passages they will find of interest.

CREATIVE & LEISURE STUDIES FACULTY   No 4

SPRING NEWSLETTER

Dear Parents and Pupils,
             In another packed term of events, the Christmas Term saw many of our pupils representing   either on the sports fields, concert platform or stage.A number of senior pupils from the School also visited the Lucien Freud Exhibition at the White Chapel Art Gallery as part of their project on 'figures'.
       The visit is part of the Art Department's policy of bringing students into direct contact with the work of contemporary artists. Another exhibition that received visits from both students and staff was that of our last Artist in Residence, Ludvic Boden. The exhibition at the Waltham Abbey Museum was extremely successful and showed the recent work which he had created at   .His sculptures are witty and highly skilled and the School should pop their heads in and admire the tremendous work our pupils produce there.Next term we will have to cope without our Head of Art, Mrs Turner, as she starts maternity leave in May. We all wish her well and news of the new arrival will be published in the Summer Newsletter. We are also happy to announce that we have secured the services of two very talented and experienced Art teachers to cover Mrs Turner's absence.
       Last Term the Music Department presented three concerts, two at the School and one at   Church. The first of these was a 'Recital Evening' in the Drama Studio. This was an opportunity for the G.C.S.E Music students to develop their performance skills prior to their examination..It was, as intended, a thoroughly enjoyable,informal and intimate evening for all who attended.There were some excellent individual performances and a wide variety of music on offer.Less than a month later the Department staged a large scale concert in the Main Hall.This was the first time for several years that the Music and P.E. Departments decided that they had enough material to fill two separate concert programmes at Christmas and reflects the healthy state of music and dance in the School.The Christmas Music Concert was a sell out and the capacity audience enjoyed a feast of seasonal music.Within a week our musicians were tuning up again,this time to present the musical parts of the   Carol Service at   Church.In just over a week thirty eight of our musicians will be sailing over to the continent on a tour to Boppard on the River Rhine.It certainly is a busy time in the Music Department,there are rehearsals every lunchtime and after school on Fridays,and we are always grateful to our core of musicians who turn up day in and day out for rehearsals no matter what the weather.Despite the additional hours Mr.Tubb our Head of Music has put in,he has still found time for some courting and we were delighted when he and Miss Godfrey,the Head of Girls P.E. announced their engagement after the half term break.
       It is a double celebration for Miss Godfrey who has recently secured the post of Head of P.E. at Woodside school in   We all wish her the very best of luck in the future,although we will miss her unbounded enthusiasm and energy tremendously.Miss Godfrey has been at the heart of the life of   School for five years and has provided great encouragement for many pupils particularly in trampolining and dance.She has also been a very active member of the Staffroom Committee arranging events such as last terms staff Quasar and bowls evening at Romford.
       Miss Godfrey's replacement will join a very active department,Mr Pepper and Miss Templeton have provided tremendous support for Mr Huizar and the extra curricular programme has been extended again this year.In last term's soccer season we managed to significantly reduce the School's P.E. transport costs by departing from the County Cup competition in the first round in all five years!We can only improve next season. At rugby,however,we have been more successful and the Yr7 team in particular finished in credit. Congratulations go to Ian Peermamode in Yr 10 who has regularly played for Essex this year as prop.Our netball team has enjoyed mixed fortunes this year with some good wins against King Harold and Burnt Mill but defeats at the hands of Roding Valley and St.Mark's.

CREATIVE & LEISURE STUDIES FACULTY
SPRING NEWSLETTER

A PACKED CHRISTMAS TERM!
Last term saw many school pupils representing ... on the sports field, on the concert platform or on stage.

ART
Several senior pupils visited the Lucien Freud exhibition at the Whitechapel Art Gallery as part of their project on 'figures' and in order to bring them into contact with the work of contemporary artists.

Several pupils and staff also visited the highly successful exhibition of the work of our Artist in Residence, Ludvic Boden, at Waltham Abbey Museum. Ludvic's sculpture is witty and highly skilled and we were extremely fortunate to have had this talented artist to inspire our pupils. ... art department is always an exciting place to visit and all visitors are very welcome.

Staff changes
We look forward to welcoming two talented and experienced teachers, covering for Mrs Turner, Head of Art, during her maternity leave starting in May. We send Mrs Turner our best wishes and hope to announce the new arrival in the summer newsletter.

MUSIC
The Music Department presented three concerts during last term. An informal and intimate recital evening, held in the Drama Studio, provided a chance for our GCSE students to develop their performance skills before their examination.

Concert
Within a month, the Music Department staged a large-scale concert in the Main Hall. For the first time for several years the Music and PE departments decided to offer separate concert programmes, evidencing the healthy state of music and dance at the School. The Christmas music concert was sold out and a capacity audience thoroughly enjoyed the feast of seasonal music.

International profile
Within a week of the concert our musicians were tuning up again, this time playing in the Carol service at ... Church, whilst shortly 38 pupils are to leave for a tour to Boppard on the River Rhine!

Commitment
It is certainly a busy time in the Music Department – there are rehearsals every lunchtime and after school every Friday. We are very grateful to all those who attend so regularly.

Music department wedding bells
Despite the additional hours he gives to the department, our Head of Music, Mr Tubb, recently announced his engagement to Miss Godfrey, Head of Girls PE, and we send our congratulations. In fact it is a double celebration for Miss Godfrey who will shortly be leaving St John's to take up the post of Head of PE at Woodside School. We wish her every success in the future although we will miss her unbounded enthusiasm and energy.

Framing data

Cramming characters on to a line, lines into long paragraphs and long paragraphs on to a page may mean we use less paper but does little for the interests of the reader. Leaving paper white can provide 'frames' for word illustrations. These frames can mean the words on the page are broken up into what can be termed 'digestible chunks' of text. Similarly, varying the lengths of paragraphs avoids the lack of interest that can occur when there is constant repetition – since the frames and the text will create 'boxes' on the page. Taking the idea of white paper frames to the extreme, if we place data into a box surrounded by white paper it can attract a great deal of attention

Can't it?

Use and return

If using photographs care needs to be taken to ensure the owner of the copyright (i.e. the person who created the photo, the actual subject rarely has any rights) is consulted and their permission is obtained for such use. If items (particularly photos) have been submitted by employees or third parties, a suitable procedure for returning the items after use should be set up. Photographs should not be written on – it is safer to use the 'post it' type of non-permanent sticky labels to provide instructions regarding use and possibly also to record the source for safe return.

Jargon

Introduction

Unfortunately for the interests of good-quality communication, we live in a jargon-ridden world. From many outlets we receive data which contain words the only reason for the inclusion of which seems to be to attempt to glorify the 'cleverness' of composition of the author. Such authors, who have overlooked the maxim 'if the reader doesn't understand it it's the writer's fault' might be less inclined to use such jargon were they to realise the true definition of the word. 'Jargon' is the description of the pleasant but meaningless sounds made by an infant (the definition of 'infant' being 'without words') before it learns to talk. In attempting to disseminate information (whether to generate a communicative process or not) we need to ensure that we avoid jargon unless we are certain that every one of our target audience will understand the language we are using.

Definition

Jargon can be described as

(a) 'the refuge of the insecure' since the author using it may well feel 'I need to protect my position and will use terms that only the privileged few will understand'
(b) 'the device of the lazy' since the author cannot be bothered to put the message in a form that can be understood by the recipient (ignoring the fact that if the recipient does not understand the fault is that of the author) and
(c) 'the response of the patronising' since the underlying or hidden message being conveyed is 'if you don't understand this why are you bothering to read it', which begs the question of the author, 'if you didn't mean it to be read, why did you bother to write it?'

How not to do it

The following examples of jargon are drawn from real-life pieces of intended communication – although it is arguable that that is the one thing they will not achieve.

Examples: Jargon obscuring clarity

1. *There is leverage there for us on the upside and there is continuing challenges for us in this environment.*

   Apart from coping with the odd use of the verb, the reader's first challenge will be to attempt to translate the sentence into English. The real problem is that if the reader realises that they will have to work hard to understand the message very often they will simply not bother to read it at all.

2. *This specially produced explanatory brochure will immediately furnish the purchaser with a comprehensive and in-depth guide to the operation, capability and accessibility of this Super Widget.*

   Minus the gobbledegook, all this sentence actually says 'this tells you how it works'. The page could even more briefly have been headed: 'Working instructions' – a description which most except the illiterate could understand.

3. *All the players in the local economy recognise that the prognosis is bleak, that complacency is unwarranted and that greater more pro-active public-sector leverage is required if the local community is to realise the area's economic potential.*

   If what is meant is 'if our local economy is to recover, the council must invest' (which is actually what the author of this local authority piece of gobbledegook intended) why not say so? Recovery will not be generated by the number of words thrown at the situation – indeed if communicating internally such an obtuse message could well be damaging.

4. *The UK recession has been a cycle of retrenchment, reassessment and restructuring for most of the operators who find themselves in our industry. We have not sought to differentiate ourselves from this general pattern and have taken active steps to preserve competitiveness and market share, despite considerable external pressures. We are in the process of conducting a comprehensive appraisal of the long-term profitability of each of our operating divisions which is leading to the termination of some products which seem to be past their peak selling capacity and this in turn is leading to a requirement for an overhaul of our staffing capacity, potentially isolated downsizing, and the assessment of the proper utilisation of group assets.*

   This is a classic example of the use of jargon and high-flown corporate phrases to try to obscure the very simple message 'We've had a tough time, which is likely to continue, and to react to the new market conditions, staff and assets surplus to current requirements are being disposed of.'

This is potentially BAD NEWS for some of those involved but it doesn't become any less bad by being concealed by jargonesque language. Indeed all that is likely to be achieved, since those that bother to read it may well be able to read between the lines, is irritation that simple language is not being used in an apparently patronising attempt to hide the truth.

5. *It is with our united and most sincere expressions of extreme regret that at this moment in time we simply cannot see our way clear to acceding to your request.*

   Translation? 'No.'

   Accepted that a one-word answer is unlikely to be used, is the recipient likely to feel any more or less disappointed if instead the reply read 'I (very much) regret that we must reject your request'?

   However, there is another dimension here. The phrase 'at this moment in time' has been used. This translates as 'now' but its inclusion begs a question. Do we mean that we have to say 'no' now but may say something different at another time? Using jargon and being long-winded can actually change the meaning of what we wanted to say.

6. *A person shall be treated as suffering from physical disablement such that he is either unable to walk or virtually unable to do so if he is not unable or virtually unable to walk with a prosthesis or an artificial aid which he habitually wears or uses or if he would not be unable or virtually unable to walk if he habitually wore or used a prosthesis or an artificial aid which is suitable in his case.*

   The patient, if persistent, reader might well feel the need of an artificial support by the time they reached the end of this 77-word sentence which might just have easily (and more clearly) been expressed by the 19-word alternative.

   If, in order to walk, a person usually needs an artificial support, they will be regarded as physically disabled.

   or the even shorter

   Those needing an artificial support to walk are physically disabled.

   Postscript: Perhaps it was using the jargon that led the drafter to infer (see original last line) that a person with such a condition might use an aid which was unsuitable!

Rules for composition

Over 50 years ago in *Politics and the English Language* (1946), George Orwell the author of the then futuristic *1984* and *Animal Farm* developed the following rules for those endeavouring to write clear English:

- Avoid using a metaphor or simile or other figure of speech which you are used to seeing in print
- Use short words rather than long words
- Avoid verbosity – cut out redundant words
- Never use jargon, scientific or foreign words if you can use ordinary everyday English words
- Always use the active tense rather than the passive, and above all
- Break any or all of the above guidelines rather than say anything that is downright barbarous!

Clarity rule

A more simple rule may be to assume that the reader is blind and since they do not read braille, the item needs to be read aloud to them. They will have no opportunity to re-read what you have written – if they don't understand it the first time round you have failed to make the piece clear.

Research

It should not be overlooked that research indicates that we only remember about 10% of what we read – the clearer the piece of writing, the easier it should be to recall it – or a greater proportion of it. Greater comprehension and recall of information can aid communication – whilst anything that impairs that will inevitably reduce the likelihood of communication being achieved.

In 1993 the *Sunday Times* and W. H. Smith jointly produced a 'One-Hour Word Power' series of handy reference books including *Word Check, Word Bank, Good Grammar in One Hour* and *Crisp, Clear Writing in One Hour*. In the last of these four titles it is recommended that simplified language should be used, substituting alternatives; for example:

Lose	Choose
as a result of	because
at this moment in time	now
come to terms with	accept
come on stream	start production
in short supply	scarce
in the near future	soon
request	ask
revealed	said
worst-case scenario	at worst

It is not difficult to write more clearly – all that is needed is intent and practice – and to spend more time during composition thinking of the interests of the target reader. It is highly likely that the more time that is spent on composition with the aim of clarity of message and purpose, the less time the reader will need to spend trying to understand what has been written.

Tailpiece – physician heal thyself

At the end of the day, our ultimate intention should be to compose carefully, a piece of information within a format where the recipient can instantly comprehend our inherent message.

> *Note:* *My last sentence would be more clearly expressed as 'The reader should be able to understand your message on a first reading'.*

Letters, memos, etc.

Introduction

Our use of the written word can be so instinctive that we can lack appreciation of what we are actually saying. A study of a cross-section of letters or memos can easily display the effect of this instinctive use of the written word – we may well discover missed points, incorrect understandings of what has gone before, poor grammar and spelling, and so forth. Why is this? Inevitably the pace of modern business life is fast – and getting faster. Hand in hand with increased pressure almost inevitably will be found an increased incidence of mistakes. Organisations may find it advisable to try to minimise the effect of this by laying down certain guidelines for the way their letters are dealt with (and indeed for making sure their letters are dealt with).

Silence invites irritation

Few things can irritate a correspondent more than a refusal on the party of their target to respond, particularly to a complaint.

Case study: Why didn't you answer?

A company found itself in an Industrial Tribunal and needing to defend an action which seemed to have very little merit. After the case had been defended unsuccessfully the company representative was chatting to his opposite number. 'Rather surprised you brought that claim – couldn't she have settled earlier?' he said. 'I don't think my client would have bothered', was the reply, 'but for the fact that she couldn't get a reply from your clients. She wrote six times and didn't even receive the courtesy of an acknowledgement – so what else was she to do?'

Key technique

Ensure all letters are answered within [48] hours.

Standard letters

In *Putting it Across* (Michael Joseph 1993) Angela Heylin suggests that most letters can be divided into the following 11 types (plus reminders):

Yes	Sorry	Can you	No
Thank you	I want	Buy my	Help
Maybe – tell me more	Congratulations	Let me explain	

If this is so (and having tried analysing my post for a few days it does seem to work for over 90% of letters) it might be helpful to provide standard letters of response so that all the respondent needs to do is to use a standard letter as a base. The operative words here are 'as a base' since the problem with many standard letters – or rather with those that seek to use them – is that laziness intervenes and standard letters are used in non-standard situations. The result is that what may have started as a routine enquiry turns into a complaint. In ARROGANCE the example was quoted of a landlord writing to a number of lessees and tenants using a standard letter. The problem was that the content of the standard letter was not applicable to the recipient whilst the tone was such that most people who received it would resent it. This may have been due to the inexperience of the writer, but the effect is to denigrate the whole organisation. In the use of standard letters (particularly when replying to customer complaints) great care needs to be exercised to ensure that:

(a) the situation being addressed really is standard
(b) the standard letter is appropriate
(c) the tone used is appropriate.

Guidelines

To ensure this is so it might be helpful for the organisation to lay down guidelines for use by those who write on its behalf.

Checklist: Guidelines for letter-writing

1. All letters are to be written on organisation letterheads using the standard layout [to be specified].
2. Only those of [status as specified] or above are entitled to write on behalf of the organisation.
3. Attention is drawn to the bank of standard letters which can be used either as drafted or as a base subject to alteration in individual

instances. On no account should a standard letter be used where the circumstances are not exactly the same as those laid down in the introduction to each letter. Where this is the case, appropriate alterations must be made to the standard letter or else an original letter generated.

4. All letters should be drafted with respect for the other party. In the event of a letter needing to be sent that criticises the other party, robustly responds to criticism by them, lodges a complaint against them, etc., such a letter must only be sent after approval by [specify] and in the exact form so approved.

5. The following points should be considered by every letter writer before a letter is sent.

(a) what is my desired result with this letter? (i.e. what am I trying to achieve?)
(b) does my draft actually deal with the point identified in a)?
(c) is my letter as clear as I can make it and will it be understood in the way I have intended by the recipient?
(d) can I reduce the length of my letter, make it clearer, remove jargon, could I make it shorter without losing clarity?
(e) what reaction is there likely to be to this letter – is that a reaction which I want?

6. No letter should be despatched without being 'spell-checked' on a word processor. In the event of the author being unsure about the grammar used, this should be checked with [name].

7. All communications sent by electronic means should comply with the foregoing (particularly 4 above). Ideally an electronic communication with a third party should be viewed by another employee before sending.

8. Copies of all letters other than routine reminders should be placed in an individual's 'Reminder' file, so that a central record exists of outstanding matters and suitable reminders can be generated after an appropriate time.

9. All letters of complaint against the organisation must be channelled through [name] although replies which must also be approved by [name], may be signed by the original person dealing with the matter.

Filtering complaints

The point of this requirement is to try to avoid the situation set out in the following case study. Unfortunately whilst empowering those low down in the organisation may be a sound way of motivating them, it can have unfortunate side effects if they are not also trained in their responsibilities.

Case study: Unpaid

The invoice was a regular one – and had never before been queried. On this occasion new staff were involved and there was a long delay. The creditor telephoned and wrote reminder letters in an attempt to discover what was holding up payment. Finally he threatened legal action. When even this prompt failed he sent a personal message to the managing director advising him of the situation and that his solicitors were ready to issue a summons. There was an instant reaction – and considerable internal investigation – since it became clear that the problem was at a level in the organisation that was not authorised to hold up payments as it had done.

Incoming messages

Obviously each organisation can only control directly its own correspondence and needs to react to that from third parties. Patience may be required here since such third parties may not exercise sufficient control over their communication material.

Case study: Oh great!

The sole trader got back to his office to find his answerphone 'message received' sign flashing. However, on playing it, he found that the machine had developed a fault and no message had been recorded. The next day he received a letter from a supplier which read 'We thank you for your esteemed enquiry of [date] ultimo in response to which we left a message on your answerphone yesterday.'

Key technique

It is a sound idea to confirm in writing that a message had been left since machines can go wrong – as occurred here. But wouldn't common sense have dictated that if you are going to take the trouble to write concerning the matter that it might have been more sensible to have   set out the message in the letter as well. As it is the trader has a non-message on the machine and another non-message in his hand – a complete information failure – let alone a communication failure. Perhaps the use of the old-English 'esteemed' and 'ultimo' prevented the writer seeing the real communication need.

Internal communication

Ideally all internal communication would be effected by employees being face to face, since that would almost certainly be the most effective method of moving matters on. Unfortunately this is almost impossible to achieve, although there are organisations (mainly those housed in one location) who have successfully outlawed the use of memos. The rationale behind action is that despite the extra time taken to walk to another's office, or to phone them, there is a higher likelihood of successful (and swifter) resolution of the matter by face-to-face discussion. At the other end of the scale is the situation existing in the organisation featured in the following case study.

Case study: What do you mean?

The organisation had experienced a problem with the production of an internal directory and found, after it had been despatched, that a number of copies had blank pages. It sent out the following memo:

> A spot check of randomly selected directories indicates that a number of such directories contain several blank pages. In view of the foregoing it is suggested that each user review his or her directory and ascertain whether or not the directory contains blank pages. In the event the directory is incomplete the user should return the directory to source for disposition.

Key technique

1. For some reason the writer dispensed with normal English and retreated (possibly as a defence mechanism because of the mistake) into some kind of 'formal reportspeak' language. However, the effect is to confuse the reader.

2. Irrelevant information is provided. How the error was discovered is of no significance to the user with a faulty directory and what the 'source' does with it is also immaterial.

3. Inappropriate language has been used. To many people the word 'review' could indicate either a musical entertainment or a request to write a critique of the faulty item, whilst asking them to 'return [it] to source for disposition' could be really confusing.

4. It fails the 'what's the point?' test. The point of the item is (presumably) to ensure that a user obtains a faultless directory – which is the one thing the 61-word material does not tell them how to obtain!

An alternative?

Some copies of the directory issued on [date] have blank pages. If your directory is faulty please return it to [name] with a note of your own name and location so that we can send you a replacement.

This 38-word message may not have reduced the word-count to the minimum that could have been achieved if the only point was a translation, but it has:

a) identified the directory more precisely and

b) told the recipient how to obtain a replacement

neither of which were addressed by the original.

Notice boards

Introduction

Most organisations use notices and notice boards. In many cases these overworked and under-cared-for workhorses may be the only source of internal information. Whether this is so or, preferably, they are part of a comprehensive information process, notices and notice boards need to be controlled carefully. Unless they are, it is all too easy for the messages of each notice to be impaired simply by the presentation of the whole board and contents. Where there is no control over the issuing of notices, most boards become swamped by paper, with the effectiveness of new material impaired by sheer weight of numbers of old notices. Old notices not only lose their effectiveness because they are well past their effective date but also tend to become 'not seen' since they have been there so long.

Challenge

The 'not seen' syndrome does not simply affect individual notices, it also affects the whole notice board. Because employees are used to seeing the board as they pass by, then that is what they do – pass by without reading. The challenge is to keep notices fresh and notice boards uncluttered so that the display captures the attention of passers-by and ensures the notices are read.

Example: Notice board control

1. Those drafting items for display on the notice boards should always remember that to be effective, such data must be written in the language of the recipient and be presented in a manner that will attract attention. Unless the notice is eye-catching it will not attract attention. Unless it is well written and clear it will not retain attention. Brevity may often aid clarity – clarity may aid effectiveness.

2. All notices should be approved for posting by [specify name] who will check that the content meets the above requirements and is in accordance with [organisation] policy.

Note: *Since the item will be posted on [the organisation's] notice board, the very fact that it is posted will imply that [the organisation] has approved the content. Someone at a senior level should therefore provide a check on this point.*

3. All notices should bear an origination date and a destruct date. The destruct date will indicate to the notice board administrator the date on which the notice can be withdrawn. No notice will remain posted after its destruct date.

4. [Specify] will act as notice board administrator and will keep a register of all notices with origination and destruct dates together with a master notice board [in Personnel Department] which should show which notices are on display at any one time.

5. All notice boards are numbered and numbered copies of each notice should be prepared to ensure that a copy of every notice is posted on every board.

6. Each week the administrator will post any required new notices and remove any notices which have passed their destruct date.

7. To aid employee recognition of the subject matter of notices coloured paper will be used.

   red will be used for safety matters

   green for disciplinary items,

   yellow for benefit-related topics,

   blue for social events and

   white for management-initiated items.

8. Notices emanating from employees and/or their representatives will be displayed on the section of each board reserved for [non-organisational] matters. However, such notices will be expected to conform to the foregoing rules and must be controlled by this procedure. They will be required to bear a destruct date, etc. No notice will be posted which is poorly presented, is in poor taste or is in any way against the interests of [the organisation]. In this respect the decision of [specify] will be final.

9. Managers and other briefers are expected to check that notices are seen and read as part of the management or cascade briefing system and to this end will be supplied with a copy of each notice posted.

Note: *It helps encourage employees to read the notices on the boards if senior managers – and particularly the managing director and/or chief executive – are seen reading them. Indeed, if personal notices are carried by the company notice boards, reading these may provide an interesting insight for the director into employees' attitudes and concerns.*

Drafting notices

A notice is a poster and needs
- to capture the eye of the beholder, by displaying a simple message with the aim of instant recognition
- to be couched in language and terms capable of being understood by the target audience, and
- to provide a contact point for further information or explanation so that any questions generated can be answered.

Case study: Pardon?

The following notice is displayed at the entrance to a local sports centre.

Please to be advised that you are now entering an area in which smoking is not permitted other than in the confines of the bar.

One member (who didn't smoke) had not visited the bar until she was persuaded by a friend. When asked why she had not visited it previously she replied that she suffered from claustrophobia and thought that the notice implied that it was 'small and poky'. The words 'confines of' had suggested to her that it was 'confined'. The notice could have been far more simply and effectively stated as 'No smoking, except in the bar' or 'Please smoke only in the bar', which would not only have had the advantage of brevity, but would also have avoided any misunderstandings because of its simplicity. In drafting notices the KISS technique – 'Keep it short and simple' – should always be remembered.

Additional guidelines

1. An eye-catching effect can be generated by using colour (either coloured paper or coloured print). Colour is a powerful indicator and if colour-coding is used it is essential that the code is adhered to at all times.

2. Notice boards should be positioned where employees pause, not where they pass. (Several organisations have notice boards in their lifts – places where employees must stop and pause.)

3. Page layout needs careful attention. Notices which present information with clear headings and subheadings, with information in digestible chunks, with clear 'attention grabbers' (headlines, subheadlines, bold text, key words, etc.) and good use of white space may well encourage more study than notices which are heavy and 'dense' with text and lack such page signposts.

4. GRAPHICS can aid readers' attention by breaking up the page and providing instant 'messages' reinforcing the text.

The power of the headline – and of the first paragraph

Headlines are often overlooked, which is the one thing that should never ever happen to them. They are far more than just a convenient lead into the subject matter and need to be given considerable attention. They should act as the initial word picture of the notice, being surrounded by blank space in order to give them prominence.

Ideally the headline should encapsulate three effects – attract attention, entice the reader to stop and read and capture the ethos of the subject matter. Since they should also be brief that is quite a challenge. Care should be taken when designing headlines for facing pages of notices. Since we tend to see facing pages as one composite picture, at least initially, if two headlines are placed next to one another on adjacent pages the eye of the reader may be encouraged to read across the combined width.

Case study: Confused?

The centre page of a newsletter displayed the following twin headlines in identical type:

COMPANIES SHOWING MORE   BUSINESS CONFIDENCE
CARING   CONTINUES
APPROACH   TO RISE
TO REDUNDANCY

It is only when one's eye reaches the middle of the second or even the third line that one realises something is wrong.

Presentations

Introduction

Research indicates that employees first preference regarding communication with or from management is a face-to-face conversation with their line manager. More formalised briefings by local management and then top management briefings and written information material are rated behind this. With a workforce of any size, however, time constraints are likely to determine that briefing presentations to up to, say, 50 employees, no matter how informal, will be more cost-effective than one-to-one conversations – indeed realistically this may be the only option. Whilst some employees are able to deal with such a challenge with ease, most find it difficult, and guidance may be required both as to the scope of the briefing and the manner of its delivery.

Research also indicates that of what people read they will retain around 10%, of what they hear they will retain 20%, but that when they both see and hear (as they do during a presentation) they will retain around 50%, and thus this means of communication is more effective than many others. Further, if feedback during the presentation is encouraged (which is necessary if it is to be most effective) then retention of subject matter may rise to around 70% – the retention level for a conversation.

Unfortunately making a presentation is thought by many to be one of the top ten most stressful experiences, which may explain why some such events are performed so poorly.

Whilst most presentations are directed towards employees, more senior managers may be obliged to give presentations to bankers, prospective investors, fund managers, etc. Many of the principles will be the same, although the informality suggested for employees may be out of place in such instances. In the following guidance it is assumed the presentations are to employees, and suitable changes will be necessary to apply the guidance to other presentational situations.

Background

To ensure the success of a presentation, those who are required to present need to receive guidance in how to manage the challenge. They should be reassured to some extent, since often the audience may be as nervous as they are. To those employees not used to such meetings, simply attending a formal briefing or presentation may be regarded as an inhibiting and ego-questioning experience. The problem then is that they are unlikely to respond even to the most earnest entreaties to participate. However, experience indicates that the more informal and relaxed such a meeting is, the more likely there is to be employee feedback and input.

This should give the presenter a clue to his/her own task:

- to make it informal, relax those present to encourage feedback and retention
- to prepare the messages required to be presented in a way that the audience can understand
- to use visual aids to help receptivity
- to provide notes to aid later recall
- to keep the tone light-hearted without being flippant, and so on.

Checklist: Presentation commitment and guidelines

1. The [organisation] wishes line and other managers to give regular briefings to their employees in order to keep them advised regarding developments, provide lines of communication for matters of concern to employees and a means by which both parties can understand the other.
2. Such briefings should be regarded as an essential part of the management and motivation of the workforce and, in order to generate a genuine two-way flow of comment, etc. need to be set up and conducted in as informal a way as possible.
3. Presentational briefings, whatever the subject, will only be effective if

   (a) the briefer is totally in command of their subject so they must ensure they prepare adequately and
   (b) the briefer gives attention to the structure of the encounter itself.
   (c) the following guidelines (see below) are observed.

Guidelines

1. Stand in a relaxed manner. In this way it is physically easy to speak and you will command attention – it is also easier to breathe deeply if you are nervous.

2. Speak without a jacket. Whilst in some instances this may be inappropriate, normally it will indicate to those present that you mean business, whilst the perceived informality may help them (and you) relax.

3. Make eye contact with the audience. Whilst this can be difficult with more than, say, 40 present, eye-contact creates rapport and enables the speaker to check receptivity. If the speaker can see that eyes are becoming glazed or puzzled (s)he may be able to recap and attempt to make the point more clearly, whilst if they become closed, an attention-gainer may be needed.

4. The room should be arranged informally – as unlike a classroom as possible. Curved or horseshoe-like layouts are preferable to straight rows. If straight lines are unavoidable setting them in a herring-bone design may break up the classroom image. In addition the herring-bone arrangement has the advantage of focusing the attention on a single central point – the position where the speaker should stand. Ideally no person should be more than 25 feet from the speaker.

5. Unless the briefer knows all the forenames of those present those attending should be asked to write their forenames on nameplates to be placed in front of them. If an employee poses a question, the briefer should then be able to use the name to personalise the interface and to aid the creation of rapport and informality.

6. Humour should be used – but only with discretion. Making employees laugh both relaxes them and makes them inhale oxygen which (at least in theory) restores their attention and offsets drowsiness. Conversely, too much laughter may belittle the presentation. However, since learning tends to be most effective when the subject is relaxed, and humour aids relaxation, this can assist. Humour also eases tension in those who find the encounter frightening. Ideally the humour should be spontaneous and arise naturally from the presentation, rather than being rehearsed. Thus humorous comments developed from the actual session, rather than jokes, are preferable.

7. Avoid distractions, both personal and within the room. Windows should be masked if they open on to an area which can provide distractions. The briefing room should not have a telephone, whilst visitors and interruptions, as well as any extraneous noise, should be avoided.

8. The room should neither be too hot nor too cold. Smoking should not be allowed – it is a distraction and an annoyance to non-smokers. Water and/or juice should be provided – particularly for the speaker as both nerves and constant speaking can dry the mouth.

9. The briefer should be able to see all those present and the audience should be able to see him/her. Notes should be provided so that

employees do not have to spend time writing these and are only required to write their own amplifying comments – if needed.

10. Simplicity should be the watchword, with jargon avoided or at least explained. The notes should be prepared and arranged in order of presentation so that everything proceeds smoothly. Nothing causes embarrassment or disruption more than the briefer being unable to find their place. Similarly all aids and handouts should also be arranged in order.

11. With smaller groups, distributing handouts of particular importance during the session can aid rapport between briefer and employees. It should also assist the break up of any formality of the session as well as concentrating the attention on the particular item. Movement (even the simple act of passing a piece of paper to one's neighbour) attracts attention – and reawakes interest.

12. Logical progression of content is essential, with appropriate links between subjects. If the order of content is unrelated, employees may become confused, and if they are confused their attention will wander. Ease of familiarity with the subject matter is all important.

13. Using visual aids will complement the briefing, add interest and encourage attentiveness. All equipment (computer display, video, slide projector, overhead projector, and so on) should be checked out and alternatives made available so that if there is a failure the disruption can be minimised. If all else fails there should always be a flip chart. Don't overuse the equipment, however – it should add interest and complement the verbal content and dialogue without overwhelming it.

14. Questions and comments should be encouraged. Again this will aid rapport and enable the briefer to check that the points have been taken on board by those present. Questions should be answered as honestly as possible, and if asked a question to which the answer is not known, the briefer should say so and promise to get back to the questioner having checked the point out.

15. Take questions during the presentation not at the end. This will encourage employees to regard the briefing as more of a conversation and less of a formal meeting.

16. In larger groups, recognise that some may be inhibited from posing questions verbally – either through a fear of speaking publicly or through a fear that the question will be regarded as 'silly'. In these circumstances, encourage the use of written questions, providing pads for the purpose.

17. At the outset stress the invitation to join in and if it is likely that questions may be slow to originate, arrange with some delegates to ask pre-determined questions.

18. Before the presentation rehearse roughly what you wish to say by speaking aloud whilst looking into a mirror. This will not only allow you to hear what the words will sound like to the audience but may also allow you to spot if you have any mannerisms of which you are not aware but which could be distracting to the audience. Listening to or watching a tape-recording or video of the rehearsal could also be valuable, although care should be taken not to be too self-critical – after all the audience will only see the presentation once and will not have the benefit of a replay button to analyse mistakes. Indeed most mistakes will go completely unnoticed.

19. It is a performance – treat it like one. Making a presentation is akin to playing a role on the stage – the speaker needs to be

- a little larger than life,
- word perfect if possible (notes can be referred to but NEVER read) and
- able at all times to make the subject matter interesting.

Case study: Attention grabbers – intended

One of the subjects on which I give seminars is 'How to write an effective report' for, among others, employees involved in administering payrolls. In searching for a way of making the subject memorable I decided to fire a starting pistol at the beginning of the presentation, asking delegates to describe what they heard. Usually after a little prompting the fact that it was a 'gun's report' was mentioned. Delegates were then asked to describe the sound, and fairly easily the descriptions 'short, sharp and provoke attention' surfaced and were written one under the other in a flip chart. Asking them which department they worked for and ringing the initial letters SSP generated the question of whether the letters meant anything to them. Obviously working in payroll departments they recognised the initials of Statutory Sick Pay but were then told that in future the letters stood for Short Sharp and Provoke attention, which were the essential characteristics of a good report as demonstrated by the gun's report. Checking retention of subject matter two years later indicated that most remembered the alternative meaning of SSP – and everyone remembered the gun's report!

Case study: Attention grabbers unintended (and unwanted)

1. The chairman was used to commanding attention and experienced in chairing Board meetings. He was not, however, used to speaking to a number of people within a more formal context. At a conference, at which

he had to give the keynote presentation, he was very nervous. This nervousness manifested itself in a habit of keeping his left hand in his trouser pocket constantly fingering a set of keys. The sound of these keys jingling was such a distraction to the audience that the impact of his words was lost. During the coffee break the discussion was more about the chairman's keys than about the chairman's words!

2. The manager was similarly unused to speaking and was equally nervous. Although he had prepared his presentation he had not delivered it out loud. The first time he heard it was when he was standing in front of the delegates. His favourite word was 'obviously', which unfortunately he kept repeating so much so that the delegates noticed the repetition and several started keeping a note of the number of 'obviouslys'. So widespread did this become that it seriously impaired the effectiveness of his presentation – the delegates were more interested in the word than the theme.

Key technique

If unused to this kind of exercise, practice is advisable in order to spot such unwelcome habits prior to eradicating them.

Problem people

Introduction

American research indicates that 94% of the population simply want to 'get along' with those with whom they interface. This leaves only 6% who are, for one reason or another, 'awkward customers' who need to be handled with some degree of care. Although 6% seems low, in the UK it could still involve 3.5 million people. Within an organisation some of these may be employees who despite what can sometimes be a great deal of effort, seem unable to either learn or improve. Ultimately it may be impossible for the organisation to continue to provide employment for such people (see DISCIPLINARY INTERVIEWS) but before it reaches that stage most responsible employers may prefer to seek to gain some improvement and to try to identify the problem and consider ways of solving it. Other 'awkward customers' are third parties over whom the organisation may have little control although some of the problems they generate are dealt with under CARELINES, CUSTOMER CARE, EXTERNAL ACTION, etc.

Identifying the causes

When dealing with problem people, whether employees or others, discovering the exact nature of their problem will assist in attempting a solution. This could involve researching as much information as possible about the person, their situation and their 'complaint' before actually seeing them. In this way, although it needs to be carried out tactfully and confidentially, a considerable amount of information may be assembled which may help identify or suggest a course of action. The following questionnaire-type checklist provides only a starting point – a meaningful dialogue with the subject may be the best way of solving the problem.

Simply researching the information may engender problems and thus it may be helpful to provide those charged with trying to solve the problem of poor performance with guidance as to the types they may have to deal with and ideas for dealing with each type as is set out below.

Checklist: Dealing with types

1. *Aggression* – try not to be provoked. Indeed if there is no reaction to the aggressive person either their aggression may disappear of its own volition, or, since such people tend to enjoy confrontation, they may in its absence abandon their attitude and go elsewhere of their own accord.
2. *Complainers* – do not be provoked. Hear them out and their complaints may cease. The danger is being seen as a sympathetic listener which may encourage further revelations.

Case study: Solved

The employee was always very vocal in her complaints about the canteen facilities, although these were usually dismissed as 'Lil's little gripes'. The newly appointed Personnel Manager invited her into her office and took note of all that she had to say, listening patiently whilst she rehearsed all her comments. A week later Lil met the Personnel Manager again and immediately complimented her on the improvements made. However, whilst the suggestions had been listed and the canteen management asked to consider them, no changes had actually been implemented.

> #### Key technique
>
> Taking complaints seriously may solve some of the difficulty in the mind of the person whose comments had previously been ignored.

---

3. *Noddys* – these are people who appear to agree to everything suggested (even nodding their heads to indicate apparent acceptance) yet do not change the manner of their approach. Such people seek to avoid confrontation so it is important to set out criticism clearly (and possibly in writing) and to gain what appears to be their confirmation that they understand what is required. They can then be shown the documentary evidence if the situation does not improve.
4. *Pessimists* – these people always believe the worst. They could be invited to imagine the worst-case scenario and effects. If suggestions of positive action can be envisaged from the worst case, action may be forced by comparison, as reality should pose less severe problems.
5. *Superior beings* – consider much of what is required as being beneath them. To deal with them the interviewer needs to prepare carefully so

that every aspect of criticism is covered by evidence and suggestions of how to improve. The essential aspects of the task and problem must be constantly reasserted otherwise the discussion will be dragged off at tangents.

6. *The indecisive* – it is necessary to discover why they cannot make decisions – are they afraid of the responsibility? If so they might be willing to move sideways – or even to take demotion. If this is not an option it may be necessary to make a written record of the requirement for decision-taking and to stress the need for timely decisions (and the negative effect of such decisions not being taken). Should the situation be repeated, the written analysis can be referred to and the consequences demonstrated as a practical effect of the inaction.

7. *Challengers* – such people fail to accept the validity of the comment. It may be impossible to make too much progress with them – although an appeal to their intelligence such as 'try it my way and see if it works, please' may at least provide evidence for the next interview.

8. *Sliders* – whoever's fault it is, 'it ain't theirs'! They need to be pinned down – again using written evidence so that the next time round the very fact that they didn't do what they said they would is self-evident. Again a written record of what was formerly agreed is essential.

Criticism

Criticism is needed from time to time – unfortunately all too many criticise too frequently and praise too seldom. However, few seem able to realise that unless the incident is handled carefully (as a means to bring about positive change) all that will result is resentment and antagonism – the result being worse than the original situation. If the culture is one where when things are done well, acceptance is the rule, but when there is a mistake it generates ill-thought-out criticism, it is hardly surprising if the latter is resented. Only constructive criticism is likely to be beneficial, and even then many people find the experience painful and possibly unacceptable. There are four main reactions to criticism: acceptance; failure to accept responsibility; failure to accept the whole basis of the criticism; and denial.

(a) *Situation and criticism accepted:* Only those who are emotionally secure, mature and committed to their own and the organisation's future may be capable of hearing and accepting criticism. Equally only such people are likely to be able to change either themselves or the status quo for which they are responsible. The critical points need to be constructed positively and people encouraged to deal with them in the same way.

(b) *Situation accepted but criticism rejected:* The subject refuses to accept responsibility for the item and 'slides' such responsibility onto others. The initiator may find it virtually impossible to pin such a person down – at least this time around (see 'sliders' above).

Case study: Non-accountability

The Chief Executive and a manager were discussing a report:

'I find it very difficult to follow this report.'

'Yes, I told my people that – but they've used the data that sales department gave us.'

'But it's your report, isn't it?'

'Not really – all we've done is to try to address the question using other people's data.'

'But you were asked to prepare this report, weren't you?'

'No, I said we could research what was available internally and assemble it for further study.'

'Right, in that case what I'd like you to do is . . .

1. As head of Development, take full responsibility for everything that's in this report and present it to the Board on [date]

2. Check all the data and the facts used and confirm that has been done

3. Add a set of recommendations as a conclusion and indicate which would be your personal preference and give your reasons.'

Key technique

The problem to be countered is that of the subject trying to 'slide away' from the responsibility. Accordingly accountability for all appropriate acts must be delineated strictly. If there is a repeat of this approach, it should be difficult for the employee to evade such responsibility – but if they do, repeat the process so that the message 'you're not going to be able to get away with this' is clearly stated.

(c) *Failure to accept the whole basis of the criticism:* Here despite critical comments being listened to and apparently accepted by the other party, there is no effect – no change to attitude, approach, etc. The criticism has been heard but is not accepted and has no effect on the status quo. Written confirmation of the standards/items/work required and a plan for action (with target dates) will be required – and needs to be policed.

(d) *Denial:* Here the criticism is made and listened to – but then denied, virtually irrespective of what can be overpowering evidence. This is indicative of a commitment to filter out criticism in order to ensure the continuation of the status quo, since the subject believes only he knows the correct way of doing things. Inherent in such a belief is of course the reverse criticism that the person seeking to alter the status quo does not understand the situation at all.

Poor performers

If a problem is related to output, exact requirements with targets, dates, etc., may need to be set and evidenced in a statement. Discussion of a failure to meet such requirements then tends to be objective rather than subjective – the person is not achieving what is required in the statement rather than not achieving what the manager requires.

Example: Policy

1. To attain its aims [the organisation] requires a reasonable amount of work of an acceptable quality from all employees on a regular basis.

2. [The organisation] recognises that at times an individual employee's performance may be less than ideal due to personal and other problems and seeks to assist people during such times by investing in the employee-assistance programme.

3. Apart from those covered in 2 above, however, [the organisation] recognises that some employees may be unable to achieve the standards required. In these instances it requires all managers, rather than invoking the disciplinary procedure, to notify [specify] who will carry out a separate investigation the findings of which will be reviewed by the manager before any further action is taken.

4. If the conclusion from the investigation is that progress is impossible then it may be necessary for the disciplinary procedure to be used.

5. If the investigation determines that there is action which can be taken by [the organisation] to assist the employee, every effort will be made to progress such action to try to solve the problem.

> *Note: It may be beneficial to have available a separate 'Capability procedure' which deals specifically with such problems without the emotive overtones of the disciplinary procedure, the use of which may generate antipathy and resentment.*

Data collection

The following checklist seeks to provide outline guidance which might be attempted internally. It is not comprehensive and is not meant to be a substitute for expert input. The key to dealing with problems is to try to ascertain the cause and asking the following questions may generate answers which themselves will provide guidance towards a solution.

Checklist: Data collection

(To compilers: Amplification and consideration of YES/NO answers is required.)

Employee

1. Is person new to job?
2. Is person new to type of work?
3. Is person new to country/part of country?
4. Has person adequate reading/speaking skills?
    a) in native language
    b) in language used at workplace
5. Is person under stress or suffering from personal problems?
6. Is person under medical supervision?
7. Are there any housing/travel difficulties?
8. Is there any evidence of disaffection regarding the department, employer, etc.? (For example the employee may have resented being passed over for promotion, or at not gaining a pay rise, or not receiving recognition for a valuable suggestion implemented, and so on.)

Training

1. Has person been present at training courses?
2. Has there been any apparent problem in acceptability on such courses?
3. Is training undertaken willingly or with apparent resentment?
4. Have courses been assessed for validity and effectiveness?

Relationships

1. Is person a loner?
2. Do they have problems relating to other employees?
3. Is there any evidence of harassment, discrimination, victimisation?
4. Has management/supervision changed recently?
5. Does employee seem to have workplace friends?

Position

1. Is position appropriate to person's skills, experience, capability?
2. Is task boring or repetitive (if so is it possible to rotate employees so that all share in this task and others which are more interesting)?
3. Are working conditions poor?
4. Are working hours unsocial or difficult?
5. Are rewards reasonable compared to other jobs in workplace, in neighbouring employers?

Notes

1. This list is not meant to be exhaustive and is put forward as a base to be customised for each organisation in each particular situation.
2. The answers to the questions will build an impression both of the employee and of the way they are fitting (or not) into the fabric of the business. Such facts should demonstrate the areas of difficulty and allow attention to be paid to these. Unless facts are available effective remedial action will be virtually impossible to implement.

Report writing

Introduction

After phone calls, letters and memos (tangible or electronic), reports must rank as one of the more widely used methods of conveying information and formulating documents of record. Unfortunately often the basic principles regarding report writing tend to be overlooked, which is very regrettable since as well as being a document of (dated) record, a well-written report can act as both information provider and discussion generator – a true communication conduit.

Basic requirements

The prime purpose of a report is to provide information to the target audience. Thus the first considerations must be to determine

(a) the information that is to be provided and
(b) the target audience.

Defining the purpose

Normally a report will be commissioned in terms such as:

'Please report on the likely effect of the proposed introduction of the new procedure for X', or

'Provide information regarding the incidence of absenteeism in the organisation and its ancillary costs, and make recommendations regarding methods of reducing both.'

It may be that the commissioning sentence is sufficient to delineate the scope of the report but if not clarification should be obtained before work begins.

Once the purpose of the report is clear this requirement should be written in large letters very clearly at the beginning of the draft report, so that each time the report is worked on its purpose is in front of the author as a reminder. Experience indicates that many reports fail to keep to the subject requested and thus fail to answer the questions posed.

Basic considerations

1. *Purpose:* All reports are commissioned for a purpose – for example to allow the Board to take a decision. In such a case the target audience is clear and the author should ensure the report is written with the requirements of (in this case) the Board always in mind.

2. *Define the target audience and present the report with their requirements in mind:* If for instance the report is for the Board, they are busy people and will not relish a bulky report, no matter how accurate the content. Thus, with such a target audience, the author would be advised to keep the report

   - short
   - sharp, and to
   - provoke the attention of the reader

(ensuring that at all times it keeps to the question posed).

3. *Recommendations:* If the terms of reference require recommendations to be made, these must be made and substantiated by the data and research included.

4. *The permanence of print:* A printed report is a permanent record of work and views and is also a permanent reflection of the author. A report which is over-wordy, rambles and misses the point reflects badly on the author.

5. *Language:* The language of the report must be that which is acceptable to the target audience. In general, ordinary everyday English should be used, as there is little chance of misunderstanding. JARGON should be avoided unless either

   - it is certain that all members of the target audience will understand, or
   - a glossary explaining the jargon is incorporated in the report.

6. *Timing:* Often the report will be required to be prepared by a certain date. A report which is late (other than for exceptional reasons) will reflect poorly on the author.

Layout

It may be stating the obvious to suggest that a report should have a beginning, a middle and an end, but experience indicates that some authors seem unable to realise that a report needs cohesion and logical progression. For the inexperienced it is helpful to generate a layout sheet indicating some pointers as to what information should go where within the report.

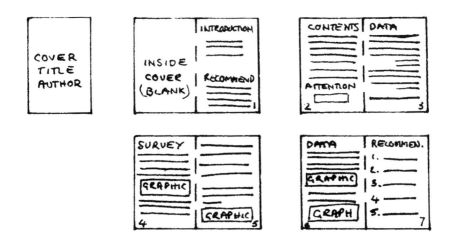

Layout sheet

In the section we can call the 'beginning' should be set the title of the report (which if carefully worded can give an instant guide to the subject matter), the author and date (which will fix the recommendations at a certain time) and the question, aims or terms of reference of the report possibly with an outline of the recommendations immediately adjacent thereto.

> Note: The value of this is that if the question originally posed is immediately followed by the answer(s) suggested, it should enable the author to check that the question has actually been answered. It may also aid readers who are short of time, as simply reading this page should give them an instant view of the purpose and conclusions of the report.

The 'middle' section of the report should include details of the research carried out and the data generated which will prompt the conclusions or recommendations. In this area there may be a great temptation to recite all the research particularly if this is substantial. However, the reason for doing this needs to be carefully examined and the question 'am I doing this because the target audience needs to see the research or is it that having carried out all this work I am determined someone should see how methodical / how much time I have spent on this /how diligent I have been in the preparation of this report?' needs to be answered. Generally the recital of full data rather than a synopsis of the salient points may not add to the report and can detract from its effectiveness since the reader's attention may decline in direct proportion to increased length.

In the end section will be the conclusion, recommendations, etc. Since the author of a report is often not present when the target audience reads it, it may be helpful not only to repeat here the outline recommendations that may have already been included in the 'beginning' section, but to supplement these with explanations which may enable the author to pre-empt the questions that the reader may have on reading the report.

Presentation

A poor report can be made to appear at least reasonable by careful presentation, but a good report can be all but destroyed by poor presentation. This is not to say that presentation is everything, but there is no doubt that, living in a visually orientated society, *how* an item is presented can 'say' a great deal about it before a word is written.

Checklist: Written presentation

1. Any piece of written material needs to seize the attention of the target audience, and then retain such attention throughout its length. The opening paragraph will set the scene for the rest of the content and it is vital that this paragraph is effective and 'attention-seizing'.
2. In these days of computer printers which are able to cram over 100 characters on a line of type, the valuable 2.5 alphabet rule seems to have been overlooked. This rule states that no line of type should contain more than 65 characters (counting as a character every letter and punctuation mark). The reason for the rule is simple: if a paragraph of more than six or seven lines is printed with over this number of characters then, without a straight edge under the line, the human eye may find it difficult to retain register on the fourth or fifth or later lines and can wander to the lines above or below. (As an example, a full line of type in this book contains on average around 62 characters.)
3. Inserting headings and subheadings, paragraph key words, or even bold type, can also help the reader to find their way to the salient points.
4. Using short but varied length paragraphs (say between 130 and 200 words) may retain the average reader's attention, whereas using long and densely presented paragraphs may not.
5. The controlled use of GRAPHICS can also aid the effectiveness of a report. Literally, since one picture can be worth 1000 words, using pie charts, bar charts and graphs can provide an instant impression of the salient points of a mass of statistics and proportions which would otherwise take the reader some time to assimilate. Any suggestion that

using graphics in place of tables of statistics is somehow patronising should be resisted – all that is being attempted is to enable the reader to assimilate the information in the easiest possible way.

6. If the report is to be printed on both sides of the page (so that page 2 appears on the back of page 1, and so on) it should be appreciated that the 'odd' right-hand pages will normally capture more attention than the 'even' left-hand pages, and that when faced with a double page the human eye comes initially to rest about a third the way down the right-hand page. Hence placing information in such a position should ensure it gains attention. To ensure the eye is directed elsewhere headings, graphics – even items in boxes (which invariably capture attention) need to be used.

7. Most reports are presented to their audience as pages clipped together with a staple. However, the simple addition of two sheets as covers (let alone anything more sophisticated), can add a great deal to the report's initial perception. Presented in this way the report gains an impression of quality – and reflects as such on the author.

Language

Whilst the way the report appears to the target audience is important, the content is obviously its most important factor. The author needs to ensure that the language is clear and unambiguous (as well as being appropriate to the target audience). It may be safest to avoid jargon and to use ordinary everyday English. The examples of confusing language in the section on JARGON should convince most authors that simple language is best. However whilst this may be true we need to ensure that the words used are interesting. Repeated use of the same verb for example can make the content uninspired and the language boring.

Example: Improper use of language

Getting up, he got his book from the shelf, went outside and got into his car and went to the library. He got out, got a free paper from the bin by the library and went into the building. He got some new books out, got back into his car and went home. He got it all done in nineteen minutes. . .

– and isn't it boring! Such boredom emanates from the repeated use of just two verbs – 'got' and 'went'. Whilst the repeated use of these verbs may be acceptable in the spoken word, when we come to write, we owe it to the reader to think more carefully about the language we use. Here the author, who wished to give the impression of speed, would have achieved his aim more effectively had he used words that themselves suggest speed, for example:

> In a rush to borrow titles before the library closed, he swiftly drove himself into town, grabbing a free paper on the way. Not bothering to spend too much time on his selection, he was back home, somewhat breathless, in less than twenty minutes.

Words such as 'rush', 'swiftly' and 'breathless' (even 'grabbing') are all indicative of movement and their inclusion gives the speed impression as well as enhancing the piece of writing generally.

In speech we do not always construct proper sentences. Indeed very often we do not finish a sentence, or interrupt ourselves, or go off at a tangent to our original intent. Whilst acceptable in (non-permanent) speech, this approach cannot be used in written communication. We need to be careful with sentence and paragraph construction – ideally keeping to simple sentences and paragraphs containing only one idea. The occasional complex sentence may be acceptable, but we should certainly avoid tapeworm sentences.

Example

Tapeworm sentences comprise complex, and, very often, long, sentences, with little bits, only loosely connected, which are intended, although they usually fail, to form one long, and usually rambling, sentence, that finishes up in a format, often very complicated, which ensures that by the time the reader, if he or she perseveres, reaches the end, they have probably forgotten the point, if there ever was one.

That is we should avoid a sentence just like the previous one, or else the reader will have the trouble it seeks to outline – forgetting the point by the end of the sentence!

Revision

Very few of us can draft a report in its final form from scratch. Ideally a report should be generated over a period of time allowing for rewrites and revisions of drafts so that it is finely tuned and polished – using the word processor to cope with the valuable second and third thoughts.

Telephoning

Introduction

So accustomed have we become to using the telephone, there is a danger that we can do so virtually without thinking. Unfortunately such familiarity can breed contempt. Thus a failure to consider exactly what we are doing and, above all, what we want to achieve, can lead us to a situation where communication is all but negated and the ultimate purpose of the call is nullified. American research indicates that only 11% of a telephone conversation may be retained with any accuracy. Hence if our aim is to impart or to obtain information we need to approach the use of the phone in a constructive way. Writing a letter requires us to consider our aim, to phrase our requests or data in a certain way, to check the wording when we finish before the other party sees what we have said. The immediacy of the phone call means that unless we make a conscious effort this preparation and thinking time may be lost and our call may be unstructured and less than effective.

Making a call

Preparation for a call is the key to successful communication by telephone and the following checklist provides a summary of the items that may require attention.

Checklist: Preparing to make a telephone call

1. *Relationship with other party*

(a) What is the history of the relationship?
(b) Have there been problems before?
(c) What information would it be useful to have available?
(d) If the person is unknown to me – what can we find out about them, their organisation, products, etc.?
(e) If they are unknown is there any way I can form a link with them (mutual interest, acquaintance, etc.) or use a third party as an introduction?

2. *Timing*

a) Is this a good time to make this call? (Phoning early on a Monday – or the day after a bank holiday – or on the first day a respondent is back from holiday, to do other than simply say 'hello and welcome back' is probably unwise. A better response may be obtained after lunch on that day or on the following day. Immediately stating that one hadn't phoned the previous day 'because I knew you'd be pretty snowed under' might also create a better rapport than otherwise.)

b) Has the respondent just returned from holiday and will (s)he be harassed and unlikely to wish to discuss the matter – particularly if it is complex or lengthy? (If the other party is known and the item is lengthy and/or complex it may be preferable to write or fax a résumé first so that the recipient does not have to come at the matter cold, and to try to improve their retention of the data.)

c) If I catch this person just as they are going home am I likely to get a quick and favourable decision, or are they likely to resent the intrusion into their relaxation time?

d) Would it be better to wait to make this call until they have received [specify] which shows us/me in a good light and they are thus likely to be receptive to my ideas?

(e) If I make this call now am I likely to time it so that it pressurises a quick decision or will it annoy them as they might suspect that is the reason I have so timed it?

3. *Purpose*

(a) What is the purpose of this call?

(b) What do I want to achieve from this call?

(c) Is the person likely to give me what I want to achieve?

(d) If so

  • do I need to tread carefully?
  • will they want something in return?
  • if so do I want to give this? and
  • if not how do I get out of that?

(e) If not – is there something I can offer which might change their outlook?

(f) What do I want to gain?

(g) Do I have anything to offer to attain the gain?

4. *Recourse*

(a) Do I need information/a favour from this person?

(b) If so what is it (list what is required)?

(c) Would it be better to ask for the information in advance so I can prepare for the call with the information?

(d) Is there information from our side which it would be helpful to give to them prior to the call to try and gain agreement and/or understanding?

(e) Is there any quid pro quo I can offer that will balance the favour being asked?

5. *Dispute*

(a) Am I ringing since we have a dispute?

(b) If so, what are the facts?

(c) Are we in the wrong (check the facts and the terms)?

(d) Who was at fault?

(e) Do we need to apologise?

(f) Is our position defensible?

- if so, how is it best defended without being aggressive?
- if not, what's the worst case and how do we avoid it?

(g) Should we have foreseen what happened?

(h) What sort of recompense is needed for:

- time
- inconvenience
- expense?

(i) Does this have potential effects elsewhere?

(j) Does it have a public relations dimension?

(k) What precedent(s) could this create?

(l) What is my scope/authority?

(m) Do I have power to deal and/or negotiate?

(n) Am I prepared to deal and finalise this matter here and now?

(o) Would I prefer time to think?

(p) Are there legal ramifications, and if so do I need advice?

(q) Do I have any conversation 'clinchers' or 'trump cards', (i.e. bargaining items) I can use to gain my desired result if things do not go well?

6. *Administration*

a) What happens if they are not there?

b) Should I compose a message in readiness to be left?

c) Do I want them to ring back or would I prefer to hold the initiative in making the call?

7. *Follow up*

a) At end of call, recap

- what we have agreed
- what we have left without agreement
- who is going to do what

(b) What have I to do?
(c) When must I do it by?
(d) What have they agreed to do?
(e) When by?

8. *Post-call assessment*

(a) Did I listen to what was said?
(b) Did I hear anything further?
(c) Did attitudes change during discussion and if so why?

Receiving

Obviously we have an advantage if we initiate the call, since this allows us the opportunity to prepare for the conversation, to determine what we wish to achieve, etc. However, we also need to receive calls – and to perfect the ability to switch our mind from what we were doing before the bell interrupted us and required us to switch attention to a subject dictated by our caller.

Checklist: Receiving a call

1. Listen to what the other party is saying (and not saying) – unless there is ACTIVE LISTENING it is unlikely that the listener will determine exactly what it is they want.
2. Don't listen in silence – silence even if meant to be encouraging can 'sound' discouraging. The use of virtually meaningless sounds – 'mmmm', 'uh huh', etc. – demonstrates that you are listening.
3. Make notes of what the caller is saying – after all if you disagree but prefer to hear them out you need to be aware of everything that you wish to contest. Only if you make notes are you likely to be sure that you can raise everything you wish to.
4. Resist the temptation to do something else at the same time, even if the caller is somewhat boring. The problem with distractions is just that – they distract attention from the caller. Indeed, if they become too interesting, this can capture the attention to such an extent that the caller realises they are not being paid attention to. Obviously this then conveys a discourtesy which can negate the meeting of minds being attempted by the call.

5. If you need to refer to other data rather than reaching for it, interrupt and explain what you want to do and then put the phone down. Unless you have a speaker-phone, the trouble with reaching for information is that you tend to miss what is being said at the time, and may even drop the phone completely!

6. If fielding a call for which you are not prepared, it may be possible to state this and to request that you ring back after you have prepared with everything you need.

7. Try to anticipate the responses of the other party to your comments and have follow-up material available so that the points you are making can be underpinned.

8. Try to keep your voice sounding friendly and the language informal. Remember that until we have video-phones the other person cannot see that you are sympathetic to their request or contentions, so it has to be done by tone of voice and by the language we use.

9. Using our title ('Mr', 'Mrs', etc.) indicates a level of formality, whereas using our first name and surname may lead to an informality which could aid the purpose of the call. Obviously such a move needs to be handled with discretion.

10. Attitudes tend to be reciprocated. If your response to a call is irritation it can tend to generate irritation in the caller.

11. When there is agreement (or even where there isn't) it can be helpful to recite the conclusions aloud (whilst making notes of them) so that both parties have a chance to correct any false impressions.

Telephiles and telephobes

The Henley Forecasting Group carried out a study in 1994 and discovered that nearly 50% of the UK population are prepared to use the phone and are confident in their use of it to carry on business. They described these consumers as 'telephiles'. Conversely only 16% are 'telephobes' – people who use the phone as little as possible. The remainder of the population don't necessarily enjoy using the phone but are prepared to do so.

During a series of communication seminars, I asked around 800 delegates to indicate who liked dealing with difficult or awkward matters over the telephone. Only around 50 (or 6%) stated that they did and, when questioned, all of them confirmed that their approach was to prepare carefully for the encounter before making the call. In most cases this involved making detailed notes of all aspects of the subject.

Checklist: Achieving short effective calls

1. Know who you need to talk to.
2. Know what it is you need to say/discover.
3. Keep preliminaries and pleasantries to a minimum (e.g. 'I realise how busy you are so I don't want to take up too much of your time' is a clever ploy to shorten a call. Few will wish to admit that they are not busy!)
4. Be brief – brief questions, brief answers, brief comments.
5. Make the call – don't take it. If you make the first move you hold the initiative and should be able to control its length.
6. Check if the time is convenient – if not arrange a time that is – don't just say 'I'll call back later' – say WHEN you will call (i.e. make an appointment for the call).
7. Listen carefully to what is said, make notes and check if there is anything of which you are unclear ('Can I just check I've got that right . . .')
8. Speak quickly but clearly and try to avoid being interrupted ('Could you excuse me for a second whilst I put this point across . . .')
9. Make notes of what was said and agreed to avoid having to ring back to check points.
10. If necessary recap what has been agreed.

Finally if the call has concluded an agreement, particularly if it was a concession from the other party, confirm your understanding of what was agreed in writing – in the event of a dispute a telephone call agreement isn't worth the paper it isn't written upon!

Temper

Introduction

Communication can only take place where there is a meeting of minds; anything that impedes this meeting will stop, or at least interrupt, the flow of communication. The less two parties have in common then the more difficult will it be for there to be communication between them. Perhaps inevitably some occasions when communication is being attempted, particularly for example when BAD NEWS is being announced, will lead to dispute, anger and to a loss of temper. When this occurs although some messages might get through it is unlikely that there will be any meeting of minds – the temper needs to be dispelled first.

Dispelling temper

It is easier to state that temper needs to be dispelled than it is actually to achieve that end. It can be extremely difficult to calm someone seized by temper, particularly as in some instances the real emotion may actually only be part of the reaction and there may be some element of play-acting for effect in the situation.

Checklist: Dealing with temper

1. Remain calm at all times. Once two tempers clash then it is unlikely that any consensus will emerge, and the situation will almost certainly degenerate.
2. Try to remind those apparently losing control that it is necessary to try to deal with matters calmly and nothing will be gained by a loss of temper. Indeed losing one's temper can probably only damage one's case. The problem is that such rational and calm comment can actually further inflame some people who almost desire their opponent to join them in the 'showdown' – 'I've lost my temper, why haven't you?' Despite the adage 'lose your temper, lose the argument', there are those who seem to enjoy a heated argument. Indeed it may be that they enjoy the rush of adrenalin that can occur when temper is lost and a verbal 'fight' ensues.

3. Note facts or opposing views uttered in temper without immediately commenting. Commenting hastily may merely inflame the situation, whilst the longer the other party can talk without being challenged, the more they may be able to reduce the pressure they feel. It is essential to try to ensure that each party speaks separately and waits, without interrupting, until the other has finished. If temper is being used for effect, then allowing the other party to speak uninterrupted may also help defuse this aspect of the problem since they may start to exhaust all their arguments. In any event they should disclose what is annoying them.

Case study: 'And?'

A famous actress was once confronted in her dressing room by an erstwhile fan who was incensed by something she had done or said (or was reported to have done or said). He berated her without letting her say anything for about a minute. At a pause she mildly said

'And . . .'

The fan continued his diatribe, often repeating himself, until he again paused for breath and again she commented softly

'And...' but the fan had had enough and rushed out of the room.

---

4. Asking neutral questions to try to uncover as much of the case, or cause of concern, as possible may help, simply from the genuine interest apparently being evinced.
5. If signs of strain continue, attempt to relax participants by allowing smokers to smoke (providing this can be done without affecting non-smokers), providing refreshments (see below) or even declaring a recess. Care should be taken not to denigrate the concern or imply that the dispute is not serious. The purpose of adjournment is to allow time for tempers to cool, for reconsideration, or thinking time, and not to stifle the matter. It may help if during the adjournment the two parties who are in opposition actually leave each other's presence, although the counter to this is that if they can share in some neutral act (see 6) the beginnings of a rapport may be generated.
6. The provision of refreshments, thereby diverting attention to a neutral and everyday shared act, may provide valuable calming time.
7. On resumption, or after any flow of temper has ceased, if no adjournment is possible, re-check and correct the facts as already

discovered and noted. This should enable a more accurate résumé of the dispute to be prepared. Further, since time will have passed since the original outburst, a more objective view may be obtained. Providing an opportunity for the antagonist to 'correct' or change some of their comments may also defuse the situation. If they do so, for example diluting the effect of previously robust statements, no comment should be made.

This process can be built upon by the note-taker tactfully questioning other facts, opinions and suppositions – and even questioning the basis of claims where these appear to be unsubstantiated.

8. Leaving as much time as possible for the calming process. Points 1–5 may require as much as 30–40 minutes. Indeed the longer the time taken the better, as the more likely it is that the temper may subside. In extreme cases it may be necessary to adjourn until a future day.

9. In making a decision under pressure, care should be taken to avoid creating precedents, and thus decisions should be of an interim nature, pending final clarification and/or approval.

10. If an interim decision is implemented a date and time should be set for review of the matter and a final decision.

Video and TV

Introduction

Movement attracts attention – which is of course one of the reasons for the immense popularity of television. The moving screen is an immediate distraction for all but the strongest-willed in its vicinity and can capture our attention in a way that a printed page rarely can. In terms of its use as a vehicle for communication (as opposed to the dissemination of information) this immensely strong enticement factor and the capacity to present an ever-increasing range of images may, however, be its only advantages compared to the spoken word and even the printed page. After all with a book or report one can re-read and re-check comments. Unless the item is recorded it is impossible to do this with a TV programme – and even if the item is recorded it is impossible to look at two 'pages' simultaneously. Further, until there is interactive TV the use for real communication (i.e. a two-way dialogue) is very limited.

Video

A number of organisations use video programmes – usually as an 'add-on' to other communication programmes, often incorporating BRIEFINGS and written documentation. Cost apart (as a rough guide a 20-minute video could cost upwards of £25,000) the use of video may be somewhat limited, although the film can provide a valuable and immediate basis for a forum for discussion. However, without the provision of the live forum (chaired by a senior manager to deal with feedback and answer queries) the video may simply generate unanswered questions. Video presentations seeking to explain, say, the financial results of an organisation, can convey general impressions better than the detail. Research indicates that relatively few people can retain detail presented via TV or video for very long, and thus to be effective such programmes may be best supported by giving the target audience a printed résumé to act as a permanent record of their messages. Videos which do not form part of a live presentation have been criticised because they cannot 'listen' – that is there is no one available to answer the questions they generate. However, if the video is an integral part of a live presentation it can add a considerable dimension to the presentation particularly if the subject of the video, often the chairman or chief executive, is 'questioned' on screen so that at least some of the questions that will immediately occur to the audience are seen to be answered, no matter how obvious it is that the questions are somewhat 'staged'.

Video presentations may become more valuable if they are used as a regular part of a wider communication programme. Thus if two or more times a year the chief executive 'speaks' to employees (or customers, franchisees, etc.) within a live presentation, the capacity to present images impossible via voice or printed page can be exploited to the full. The danger may be that because of the expense, should other priorities take precedence and the budget for such items suffer, the effect on the target audience of losing the (perhaps) more entertaining part of their presentation may be severe.

Television

The problem that video, audio tape and the printed page all share is that although they can present information they cannot of themselves answer original questions that such information generates from the target audience (whether internal or external). Similar problems arise with the use of television, although technological advances or the use of the telephone or e-mail with a live television presentation, may enable what is primarily another means of providing information with the possibility of generating a true communication process.

Case study: Car wars

Vehicle manufacturer BMW uses television (via satellite transmission) to inform their staff in over 140 dealerships the latest information regarding sales, marketing, data on competitors and so on. Since the programmes are developed weekly and edited overnight, the immediacy of the news is stated to be very valuable. However, the company realised that whilst of considerable benefit, the messages were only flowing one way, and refined the system so that staff were able to phone up during 'live' sessions and ask questions of executives 'on screen'.

Key technique

Getting the information to the recipient is a problem, but one which is usually solvable with determination and ingenuity, even if the time parameters are tight. The real test is trying to turn a single-track, one-way, information-dissemination process into a dual response process – thereby converting information into communication.

Obviously those taking part in an interactive process like this will need to be fully briefed since, unlike the 'staged' questions that may have been featured in a video presentation, they are going to be faced with real live and potentially searching questions. However, this should be no more of a problem, other than that the audience may be larger, than will be the case where a senior manager is making a BRIEFING to employees and encouraging feedback. There is one important difference, however – the audience is unseen and thus the person providing the answer cannot gauge the reaction of the audience to the question – or to the answer. It is relatively easy to assess how the audience has viewed a 'personal presentation' (i.e. one where audience and presenter are face to face) simply from the attitude of the audience during the 'show' and the tenor of their questions. If seeking to assess the reaction of a TV audience, there may need to be a survey or questionnaire for the whole or a sample of the audience.

Case study: Getting some extra help – the Halifax TV experience

Problem: How do you contact 37,000 employees at 1,700 units of the largest Building Society in the world, when they are spread throughout the country, so that they receive the same message virtually simultaneously and can also be encouraged to respond and interact with those conveying the news?

Answer (according to the Halifax): Set up and use your own in-house television service. The service, which added a dimension to the existing regular paper-based employee communication data, cost £5 million, most of this being the cost of the installation of satellite receivers and television and video equipment at all the society's outlets.

A team of ten, headed by Business TV Controller, Martin Batt, produce around 60 programmes each year including a fortnightly business news service aimed at all employees, plus a monthly programme which is specifically for sales and marketing staff.

Although each script is produced by a team of five in-house writers, the programmes use professional presenters who not only report news but also interview managers on a range of subjects. The response to the new service has been enthusiastic, with most employees ranking Halifax TV equal in value to a face-to-face briefing with their immediate manager (ranked in MORI's research to be employees' most preferred means of communication) whilst tested receptivity is extremely high (85–90%) in the branches. The service proved of considerable value after the Halifax merger with Leeds Permanent Building Society since key issues could be explored and opportunities and challenges explained.

Traditionally TV allows information to be disseminated from source to audience only, but Halifax has experimented with phones which allow members of the audience to pose questions to the presenters and interviewees. 'The problem there', comments Martin Batt, 'is that you need a long programme to allow time for the audience to assimilate what is being said, and then to consider and pose questions. We have also trialled interactive key pads which enable questions to be posed directly to the presenter by the audience in the branch network.'

Care is taken to brief managers first concerning big news stories (branch reorganisations, changes to terms and conditions, etc.) so that the line of command is preserved. Other than that the local staff watch the programmes as a team – a situation which also allows managers to deal with local matters at the same time. Regular checking is conducted to test staff reactions. After each programme a sample of 40–50 employees are contacted to gain their reaction and in addition four times each year a sample of 500 employees are tested on their receptivity. So far the response has been extremely good and there is no doubt that the programmes are fulfilling a clear communication need.

Problems? Martin Batt comments, 'It can be easy to be dazzled by the technology, which can have a negative effect. It is after all the message which is important rather than the means of conveying the message. A poorly delivered message on TV can be damaging – in some cases more damaging than the lack of a message altogether. We therefore put a lot of emphasis on planning and preparation to ensure we get it right – at least most of the time!'

PART 2
Challenges

Aims

Introduction

Experience indicates that many, including senior management as well as those at lower levels of responsibility, connected with organisations do not fully appreciate the aims of their businesses. To ensure that all connected with the organisation understand what it is about, and to provide a sound criteria for actions, an increasing number of employers are codifying their aims and having done so, promulgating them as an integral part of their information/communication material.

Strategy

The strategical thought behind the adoption and promulgation of aims is that

- all those working with and for the organisation, as well as those coming into contact with it, will have a clear idea of its purpose
- without such aims management and employees (particularly) may have an incomplete understanding of the reasons for the requirements placed upon them
- with the adoption of such aims clear criteria exist to act as guidelines in all aspects of the organisation's operation and business.

Examples: Organisation aims

Our aims are to

Example A

1. Increase profit and productivity for the mutual benefit of customers, employees and shareholders

2. Give complete customer satisfaction and have a proper responsibility to the community

3. Provide opportunities for each employee to develop his/her capabilities

4. Foster better communication between management and

(i) employees (ii) customers (iii) suppliers (iv) shareholders (v) the local and national communities

5. Develop better understanding, develop decision-taking and encourage accountability

6. Recognise the individual importance of every employee.

Example B

1. To provide our customers with the highest standard of product and service at a fair price

2. To provide our employees with the security of working for a successful company with job satisfaction, a good level of remuneration and working conditions, acknowledging their right to be informed and consulted on all matters affecting their employment and work

3. To earn sufficient money after tax to provide an adequate return for our shareholders, having invested enough capital in the business to maintain the value of the shareholders' assets and to ensure the long-term growth of their company

4. To conduct our business with due care for the community, the environment and for the interests of the consumer and the general public.

Example C

1. To provide reliable and quality products and services to our customers, giving value for money at all times

2. To create wealth for our owners, and wealth and long-term steady employment for our employees

3. To provide opportunities for employees to develop their skills and talents to the extent that they wish

4. To foster communication between all involved in the organisation

5. To be responsible members of the community, carrying on our operations with respect for neighbours, state and the environment

6. To abide by all obligations – including national, local and industry specific laws, regulations and rules.

Use and perceptions

The advantages of a genuine and ongoing commitment to such aims are

- the directing body of the organisation is confirming (informing) the ethos that exists here
- objective criteria (rather than subjective judgements) exist as a measure for variations from requirements
- actions and attitudes which do not accord with the aims can be identified (and thus rectified) – thus clear parameters for action are determined.

The perception of the directing body of an organisation can vary depending on the observers, be they employees, suppliers, customers, shareholders, neighbours, etc. These perceptions will depend initially on the strategy that the directing body of the organisation adopts, and then on the information and messages that flow from the organisation. Thus all items of information need to reflect the lead given by the wording of the aims.

Writing in *Communicators in Business* in summer 1996, Jane Ferguson, Managing Director of public relations consultants Burson-Marsteller, stated 'whatever words you use to describe it, the perceptions of a company by key audiences are a powerful force. These perceptions influence the behaviour of employees, customers and shareholders, and that behaviour is what makes the difference between success and failure in a company's attempts to meet its business goals.'

Aims act as a measurement criteria. Attitudes, rules, decisions, etc., made in the course of business can be compared with their ideal. The criteria are available for all those having a stake in the organisation

- managers (demonstrating how they should deal with similar problems in the future)
- employees (indicating the kind of treatment or reaction they can expect in similar circumstances)
- shareholders (evidencing the corporate commitments of their company)
- customers (in terms of the regard in which the organisation holds their custom)
- suppliers (in terms of the value placed upon their contribution to the success of the organisation)
- the community (in terms of the endeavour of the organisation to act responsibly with appreciation of the value it derives from the community).

Public accountability

The various audiences outlined above cannot be compartmentalised and dealt with individually – they are inextricably intertwined. For example, employees can also be shareholders, customers, members of the public and residents in the community. Similarly, customers can be residents in the community, shareholders and members of the public, and so on. The organisation needs to stress to those responsible for conveying its messages that they are all responsible for interfacing with all the stakeholders and in accordance with the aims.

Since every action, decision and pronouncement of most wealth-creating organisations is increasingly subject to scrutiny, all such items need to be assessed for ultimate effect. Those responsible for the decisions and their promulgation need to consider the effect of such decisions on the perceptions of all interested parties. (See COMMUNITY RELATIONS, PUBLIC RELATIONS.)

Communication in this regard needs to be continuous. Equally, most people are far more ready to listen to and to accept bad news rather than good. Unless organisations are ready to provide information they can find that bad news based on rumour is more readily believed than good but accurate news. The Greek philosopher Phocion said 'the good have no need of an advocate', but nowadays this is probably not so.

Annual General Meeting

Introduction

A company's Annual General Meeting (particularly that of a listed company or one with shareholders who are not directors or members of their families) is usually the sole occasion in the year when the corporate entity is 'on display'. For that reason careful planning is needed to ensure, as far as possible, that the company is seen from as advantageous a perspective as possible, as this will convey a powerful message to those attending the AGM (and those to whom they speak). This will require careful planning and attention to detail. The interim report of the Hampel Committee on Corporate Governance recommends that Boards should be prepared to make a presentation at the AGM covering their business plan.

Planning

The following checklist provides a base to be customised. If, as seems increasingly the case, pressure groups are expected to attend, adequate defensive measures may also need to be incorporated.

Checklist A: Initial considerations

1. Prepare list of all items needing to be addressed (see Example below)
2. Allocate responsibilities with timing requirements
3. Ensure all those delegated such duties understand requirements and the importance of the company being seen to be in control and in a beneficial light
4. Check all preparations one month prior to event
5. Consider style/content to be adopted with chairman/Board
6. Consider whether pressure groups/hostility is expected
7. Consider whether poll likely to be demanded and, if so, make arrangements for taking poll
8. Obtain advice on difficult questions which might be asked
9. Prepare draft press release to follow conclusion of meeting.

Example: General administration

Item	Responsibility
Decide date and time	Board
Visit venue, check facilities	Co. Sec./Board

Book venue (6–12 months ahead) – check: Co. Sec./Board
- room and overflow facility
- air conditioning/ventilation
- acoustics/amplification
- accommodation including catering/toilet facilities
- notice boards/room directions
- tables for signing in

If product/photo display required: Marketing Dept
- display tables/video/computerised programme

Stipulate to venue management: Co. Sec.
- timetable for arrivals
- serving tea/coffee
- lunch (if required)
- likely departure

Delegate items to staff: As allocated
- greeting arrivals
- ensuring arrivals sign in (taking attendance card)
- ushering to seats
- care of Registers and Proxies
- acting as teller(s) (in event of voting on poll)
- care of statutory books, service contracts, minute book
- liaison with catering
- spare copies of annual report, publicity handouts
- checking those who are to propose/second resolutions are present

Arrange 'proposers and seconders':   Co. Sec.
- 'tame' members (and back-up in event of absence), who will actually propose and/or second the various resolutions to avoid it looking like too much of a one-person (i.e. the chairman's) show

Anticipate and prepare for any hostility:	Chairman
• liaise with advisers	
• preparation of answers to awkward questions	
If chairman requires a brief:	Co. Sec.
• preparation of brief (i.e. a script to cover each part of the meeting)	
Publish timetable and checklist:	Co. Sec.
• briefing on preparations, likely problems, etc. (i.e. a meeting scenario) for Board and advisers	
Liaison with:	Finance Director
• auditors (must attend and will usually read Audit Report)	
• solicitors, stockbrokers (for PLC)	Co. Sec.
• public relations (and, through them, media representatives)	Corporate PR
• company registrar (including printing of dividend cheques and tax vouchers, and arrangements for granting authority to post)	Co. Sec.
Make transport arrangements:	Transport Manager
• for directors, staff, guests, major shareholders, etc.	
Arrange for:	Director
• display of products/tour of premises	
Press release:	
• if required post the event, draft and agree with chairman in advance, possibly amending should this be required following any developments at the meeting	Corporate PR

Board support

Ideally the meeting should proceed smoothly even if this gives the (accurate) impression that the whole thing has been stage-managed. This will mean that each resolution should have its own proposer and seconder already identified. Further the Board will wish to know at an early stage whether any item of business is likely to be subject to challenge. For that reason if few shareholders (or those commanding a small proportion of votes) are likely to attend it may be necessary for the Company Secretary to contact friendly shareholders to obtain their proxy votes. As proxy cards arrive, they should be totalled so that at the beginning of the meeting the chairman has full details of the support (and opposition) for each resolution.

Hostility

If hostility or antipathy is expected the steps set out in Checklist B should be considered.

Checklist B: Reaction to hostility

1. Identify source and extent of support
2. Ensure 'hostiles' do actually have a right of attendance and ensure they are barred if they do not have such a right
3. If time allows, consider possibility of a private meeting to discuss matter to try to avoid public confrontation
4. Monitor arrivals – arrange for security to be ready to deal with any disruption either on arrival or during the course of the meeting
5. Canvass proxies sufficient to ensure overcoming opposition
6. Prepare a list of the questions least wished to be asked – and a crib of suitable answers
7. Brief the directors concerned of the source of the problem and the steps taken to control/deal with it
8. Brief media contacts and provide media trained spokesman to answer follow-up queries (see PUBLIC RELATIONS)
9. If the hostile shareholder wishes to make a point s/he should be allowed such a courtesy, answering the points made as far as possible and offering subsequent discussions if this is feasible.

Communication material

Several documents need to be produced if the business of an AGM is to proceed smoothly.

(a) *Notice:* Although the Notice of the Meeting is usually included in the ANNUAL REPORT there is no reason why this could not be sent separately. An increasing number of PLCs do send the notice, with an informal letter which often invites shareholders to the meeting, which explains the significance of complex business that will be discussed and so forth.

(b) *Letter of invitation:* The letter accompanying the Notice may also urge private shareholders to attend the AGM.

(c) *Intention and Attendance cards:* Companies with large numbers of private shareholders, many of whom may wish to attend the meeting, often send 'intention' and 'attendance' cards. Shareholders are urged to return the 'intention' cards in advance (to give the company some guide to the possible numbers attending), whilst using the 'attendance' cards when they arrive at the meeting may enable large numbers of attendees to be processed swiftly (it also aids security screening). Obviously no shareholder without a card should be barred from entry – processing their entry will simply take more time.

(d) *Proxy:* Proxy cards will normally have been sent with the Annual Report and/or Notice of Meeting. These are required to be lodged with the company before the meeting and should be checked and an analysis of the support and opposition applicable to each resolution passed to the chairman before the meeting. The proxy forms themselves should be available at the meeting. Those processing attendance need to be able to cross-reference the proxies with the attendee list, in case a person who has already lodged a proxy attends in person.

Receipt of a proxy form should be regarded additionally as a source of up-to-date information, for example regarding addresses (although a 'change of address' slip can also be printed as part of the dividend voucher).

Informal communication

Since such meetings tend to be fairly formal, some PLCs arrange for members of the Board to make themselves available at the AGM venue, say, 30 minutes before the meeting (and/or for a time afterwards) so that shareholders can talk directly to them. The advantage of this facility being used to try to 'draw' any hostility from the more public domain of the meeting should not be underestimated, although directors may need to be cautious regarding their comments to avoid disclosure of price-sensitive material which could infringe the insider-dealing legislation. For non-public companies the AGM is likely to be a less formal event and such informal contact can be achieved relatively easily.

The script

Obviously the chairman (and any other director expected to address the meeting) should be well versed in all aspects of the business and questions relating to it. As detailed in the above checklists it is essential that there is adequate preparation for dealing with awkward questions – in fact that the speakers 'sing from the same song-sheet'. In addition those not used to handling potentially hostile questions may need training in such tactics. To some extent 'hostiles' may feel that they will maximise the achievement of their ends by generating hostility in return since such a spectacle may be featured by the media. The need for adequate preparation and calm in the face of hostile questioning is essential. Even if hostility is not expected or evidenced the need to present the management in as competent a light as possible will require similar attention.

The future

Business and employment is increasingly subject to legal requirements and, moreover, to scrutiny by the media. Such scrutiny is not purely to report to absent shareholders, but mainly on behalf of employees, the community and consumers. Similarly, it will not simply consider the financial results, but examine a company's safety records, its attitude to charity, its record on environmental issues, and so forth. General meetings are an obvious focus for comment, and attention is needed to ensure that during and after such events it is the messages the company wishes to convey that are those the public receives. Equally companies need to listen to the feedback such reports generate. As Anita Roddick (founder of The Body Shop) said recently, 'Business leaders have a choice – they can either build a public relations wall, or they can listen and respond. Will they build more smokescreens and inertia or will they listen and act? Consumers will be watching.'

Annual report

Introduction

A limited company is required by law to provide a report each year to its owners. For many this is the embodiment of shareholder information – not communication as few may be able, or even invited, to provide feedback unless they attend the AGM. Being required to produce such a report in turn provides an opportunity for the company to promote itself and its results. Considerable thought needs to be given to the production of such a report – not only to ensure compliance with the legal requirements, but also to ensure accurate 'messages' concerning the company are provided for all interested parties.

Determining the point

The purpose of such a report is

- to provide an accurate guide to the financial state of the business (over a set period and as at a particular date) and
- to give an account of the stewardship of the directors to those who appointed them – the owners or shareholders.

However, current practice is to design such a report to cater for the attention or requirements of a variety of other audiences – the stakeholders referred to in AIMS. In short there is an opportunity to use the report for PUBLIC RELATIONS purposes. Even the reports of private companies which lack the high profile of listed PLCs, may be required for bankers, lenders and prospective shareholders. Thus the ultimate audience may be wider than initially thought.

Checklist: Audiences for annual report

1. Shareholders – private, institutional and prospective
2. Stock exchanges
3. Analysts
4. Mailing list

5. Advisers, brokers, media
6. Government agencies, local and national politicians
7. Accounting professions
8. Creditors, lenders, developers, customers, landlords, etc.
9. Employees (current and retired)
10. Recruitment agencies, schools and universities
11. Trade unions
12. Pressure groups
13. Archivists and libraries
14. Competitors

Required information

The preparation and filing of a Report is a legal requirement, but reporting results should not be simply a matter of complying with company law and accounting regulations. Business is about confidence and, particularly for a public listed company, the reporting of results is an important facet of the building and sustaining of confidence. The tone, quality and presentation of the annual report says a great deal about the company, and for this reason, if no other, care needs to be exercised when considering the content of statements of the company's achievements.

Reports that merely comply with the legal requirements tend to be unattractive, and may be regarded by many as virtually unreadable, except by the very determined and expert. The following list of a report's other purposes may put its production in perspective.

Checklist: Additional purposes of annual report

1. *To explain purpose and strategy:* Companies' aims, tactics and strategy are easily misunderstood unless constantly reiterated and updated. The annual report (particularly the statement by the chairman) is ideal for this, giving considerable scope for detailed explanation.
2. *To give information:* Companies can remain largely secretive concerning their operations and/or products, and this may at times be understandable from a self-preservation view. The inclusion of general information, when not 'competitor-sensitive' can, however, aid the products' own marketing and certainly aid the reader's comprehension of the company.
3. *To aid press coverage:* The report forms the backbone of the financial journalists' reference file from which their 'stories' will draw much of their background material.

4. *To encourage confidence:* The share prices of public companies are often highly sensitive. A well-produced report containing decent results and bullish forecasts or commentary can help support the price of the company's shares.

Theme

The various aims and audiences of an individual report will vary from company to company and from time to time. The aggressive conglomerate growing by acquisition may wish to use a high profile image, although conversely at times it may need to 'dampen things down' whilst secretively stalking a particular prey. The high street chain store may have (and wish to sustain) a higher awareness profile than a similar-sized manufacturing company. The newer 'high-tech' industries tend to have a higher profile than the older, more established companies, and so on.

The relative importance of each aim needs to be assessed and built into a theme to which constant reference should be made to ensure the impression given by each item (particularly if these are written by several authors) is consistent, and that illustrations and pictorial inserts similarly reflect the same 'message'.

Style

There can be no hard and fast rules concerning the design of corporate communications, other than the fact that the style of communication should reflect the style of each individual company at that particular stage of its development. Above all, however, a report should seek to *explain* the results and the strategy in simple everyday language – and this aim of explanation should be tested from time to time by surveying the audience. Too many corporate reports leave all but the qualified accountant numb with incomprehension, and perhaps private shareholders annoyed at the wastage of company resources in producing what they perceive to be a largely unintelligible document. Research has suggested that many private shareholders (being non-financially expert) can actually gain much of their appreciation of the progress of their company and of the salient features of the results, by reading an EMPLOYEE REPORT rather than by studying the annual report. Both in writing and in presentation clarity and lucidity should be watchwords.

Planning

A report must be produced to a strict timetable, relating as it does (at least for public listed companies) to fixed dates for the preliminary announcement, Stock Exchange notification, posting date, dividend striking date, and so on. The preparation of a timetable in consultation with all involved – accounts staff, auditors, share registrar, advisers, designers, typesetters, printers, those responsible for mailing and distribution, etc. – is essential. Not only should this timetable cover deadlines for each aspect of the production but also it should allow for the insertion of the initials of those responsible for individual aspects.

Example: Report preparation timetable

Item	Timing (Note: D = despatch date)	Executive(s)
Prepare budget	D –100	Co. Sec./Fin. Dir.
Prepare timetable (in liaison with ghostwriter/designer/typesetters/printers)	D –90	Co. Sec./Fin. Dir.
Rough mock-up of report	D –80	Designer/Fin. Dir.
Board agree budget and mock-up		Board
Chairman's statement, 1st draft		Ghostwriter/ Chairman
Executives' reports, 1st draft		[Initials]
Proxy and other cards (e.g. AGM attendance and admittance cards), 1st draft		Co. Sec.
Chairman's statement, etc., 2nd draft	D –80	Ghostwriter/ Chairman
Analyse numbers of reports required	D –70	Co. Sec.
Advise printer so that paper can be ordered		Co. Sec.
Photographer/illustrator commissioned and instructed		Designer/Co. Sec.

Chairman's statement, final draft and copy to printers/typesetters	D –60	Ghostwriter/ Chairman
Liaise with registrars and provide checklist	D –50	Co. Sec.
Liaise with corporate public relations		
Liaise with brokers		
First proof back, checked and returned to typesetters		Co. Sec./Auditors
Second proof to company/auditors	D –40	Co. Sec./Auditors
Photographs/illustrations reviewed and agreed		Chairman
Third proof (colour)	D –30	Co. Sec./Auditors
Preliminary announcement	D –25	Co. Sec.
Insert figures in third proof for typesetters		Co. Sec.
Commission dividend warrants		Co. Sec.
Final proof checked	D –15	Chairman/Co. Sec.
Print order given. Printers liaise with registrars to collect envelopes and despatch	D –10	Printers/Co. Sec.
Report despatched externally	D –1	Despatch
Report distributed internally	D –day	Co. Sec.

Notes: 1. Whether the Chairman (and other executives) write their own statements or have them (or at least an initial draft) written by the Company Secretary or a professional ghostwriter needs to be determined. A number of such statements are written externally, one advantage being that the ghostwriter will tend to see the company as would the external market and can express the statement accordingly. Conversely many chairmen prefer to write the statement themselves so that it bears their own style. A compromise may be for the ghostwriter to compose the first and second drafts, leaving the Chairman to customise and style it.

2. If also preparing a Summary Financial Statement and/or an Employee Report – either as separate documents or as one or more sections within the report, the timetable for preparation of these one or two additional item(s) needs to be interwoven.

3. Since the Annual Report of most public listed companies incorporates the Notice of the Annual General Meeting, the Company Secretary will need to relate all requirements in that regard – booking the venue, arranging the event, ensuring the report is posted and gives sufficient notice, etc. – to this timetable.

Layout

Seldom will the opportunity arise to design such a report from scratch and in many instances companies are content to 'follow last year' by simply altering last year's copy. Production may be rendered relatively easy in this way although inevitably the report may lack originality.

The preparation of an outline pagination chart (see below) will aid in this respect since it requires the person responsible to plan the production well in advance of the timetable and to obtain quotations, as well as helping with the more mundane task of deciding what 'feature should go where'.

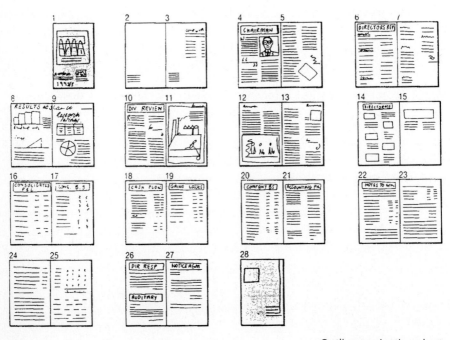

Outline pagination chart

If this outline content check is used and early decisions are taken regarding size and type of graphics and the font and size of type to be used, this will help determine the number of words required from each contributor. Since, almost inevitably, contributors tend to write too many words and to deliver them late, a text length somewhat shorter than the required length should be requested some time before the real deadlines (i.e. those shown in the timetable). If text is too short the problem may be overcome by increasing the sizes of illustrations or adding headings and subheadings, etc. Text which is too long should be edited by (for example) the chairman.

Design

Considerable value can be obtained in comprehension and presentation by taking an objective view of layout, style and content of the report, even if the expense of retaining a designer is felt unnecessary on an annual basis. Investing in an externally produced design in year one which is then used for the next three or four years may prove to be cost-effective.

Until the advent of the UK recession of the early 1990s, many corporate reports had become increasingly lavish and glossy, reflecting in many ways the hyper-confidence of their companies and the economy. Such reports reflected the trend to designer fashions particularly of high street retailers, or companies with high-profile consumer products. They were often accurate ambassadors for their companies at that time and achieved most of their purposes in simply enticing the reader to open them and browse. In recent years and particularly as a result of the recession dampening confidence, the trend to such 'designer' and glossy reports has faded and they now tend to be more workmanlike. In many respects the discarding of the former 'hype' may be welcome if it allows concentration on the essentials. Nevertheless, since the annual report is the one document of record issued by the company in the year, it needs to be presented in a way that reflects the company's aims and aspirations as well as its underlying achievements and results.

Adding enticement

In many respects, the promotion of the company can be achieved by the incorporation of items other than the financial results themselves. Thus the text must be easy to understand and, in requesting contributions from executives, they should be asked not just to write a certain number of words in decent ordinary English (avoiding JARGON, 'buzz' words and the like) but also to suggest complementary illustrations. Illustrations in this context does not just mean photographs, as graphs, histograms, bar-charts and pie-charts all have a part to play. If using such items, their compilation and incorporation must be subject to certain rules and guidelines. See GRAPHICS.

Gaining acceptability

In considering reporting to shareholders, the concept of using an EMPLOYEE REPORT and/or a SUMMARY FINANCIAL STATEMENT as an additional means of communication should not be overlooked – after all the aim should be to ensure that those who receive reports are able to understand them. In fact research indicates that only about 5% of the target audience actually read and understand their companies' annual reports. If the reader doesn't read it, the responsibility can only be that of the author.

Case study: Not our fault

It is stating the obvious to suggest that the content of an annual report should be accurate. However, mistakes are made. In the report of one listed company was a page of graphical representations of six statistics which sought to show the progress of the company. That there had been progress was beyond doubt. However, each graphic overstated the amount of progress in an area to a considerable extent. When this was pointed out to the Chairman the response was 'Oh, we leave that to the designers.' This may have been accurate but the responsibility for publishing misleading data is that of the directors – ironically within a year the company was in serious financial difficulties. Too casual an approach to published statistics had been echoed by a similar arrogant and casual approach to budgeting and financial control – the fish rots from the head.

Bad news

Introduction

Almost inevitably an organisation will need to deal with the promulgation of bad news at some time during its life. Where the dissemination is required externally the suggestions made under CRISIS COMMUNICATION are appropriate. Even where the news is wholly related to internal matters, it may be necessary to consider the external implications – COMMUNITY RELATIONS where the organisation is a large employer within a small area. However, the main consideration should be to ensure adequate communication with those directly affected. Perhaps the most obvious example would be a requirement to lose staff via redundancy (the example used below) where both those who are to go and those who are to stay should be informed before any other interested parties. Whatever the nature of the bad news, ideally the person responsible for communicating it should attempt to put him/herself in the position of the recipient and ask, 'If that was me:

- what would I want to know
- how would I like to be told
- how would I like to be treated?'

Redundancy

Whilst it should be the aim of every employer at all times to maintain full employment for all employees, since it is impossible to forecast product demand at all times, it is also impossible to guarantee full employment, and an employer should never guarantee that there will be no redundancies. Few people are foolish enough to believe that such promises are unlikely to be broken – breaking the credibility of those that made them as well as the guarantee itself. It is far more sensible to adopt a redundancy policy. Legally employers who make more than 20 employees redundant within a period of 90 days need to consult their elected representatives. It may minimise the emotive reactions that inevitably result once the word redundancy is mentioned, if:

(a) a comprehensive redundancy policy is agreed and

(b) elected representatives (possibly using those elected to a JOINT CONSULTATIVE COMMITTEE (JCC) or Works Council as such representatives) are available.

The draft procedure set out in the following checklist could be used as a base for action. This is important since in following the various steps communication which is essential in such circumstances will start to flow.

Checklist: Outline redundancy procedure

1. Prepare a policy wording which covers all the items set out below. Ensure it is made readily available to and accepted by all employees.

2. Agree who are to be the employee representatives – ideally with deputies in case the elected representatives leave.

3. When a reduction in employee numbers seems likely, advise all employees that this situation is likely to arise and redundancies are anticipated.

   Note: This is not notification of actual redundancy but an indication that this could arise. With the benefit of consultation and communication the ideas and suggestions of those with most to lose can be generated which may avoid the need to cut jobs.

4. If trade unions are recognised then consultation must take place with them for set periods. These periods are 90 days if 100 or more employees are to be made redundant over a period of 90 days at a single establishment, or 30 days if 10 or more employees are to be made redundant over a period of 30 days.

   The Department of Employment must also be notified.

   Note: Where there are recognised trade unions their elected shop stewards may act as elected representatives for the purposes of redundancy consultation; however, the choice of whom to consult belongs to the employer.

5. Elected representatives will be consulted regarding the extent of the redundancies, its reason, the proposed method of selection for redundancy, terms, etc.

   Note: Again, seeking the views of employees may engender surprising and innovative suggestions – including a pay reduction for all to avoid the redundancies of the few.

6. The basis of selection must be fair and objective to all involved.

7. Individual performance (absenteeism, attitude, disciplinary record, etc.) can be taken into account provided that all records are suitably and

objectively scrutinised.

8. Employees will be invited to volunteer for redundancy, making it clear that the requirement to retain suitable skills to run the operation may result in some offers being rejected.

9. All employees volunteering and being selected for redundancy should be given a letter confirming the fact and the amounts payable on their termination (including redundancy amount, wages and holiday pay to leaving date, any payment in lieu of notice should the full statutory or contractual, if longer, notice not be given, less any reductions for loans, etc., repayable to the employer).

10. Once the required number of job reductions has been agreed and the number of voluntary redundancies is known, jobs – and the job holders to make up the difference – must be identified.

11. Individual consultation will take place with those selected. Alternative suggestions made by those selected will be considered.

   Note: *Although there is no legal requirement for such individual consultation, custom and widespread practice create pressure for this to occur. Tribunals may tend to regard a lack of individual consultation as unfair. Where the numbers to be made redundant are fewer than 20 (i.e. so that consultation with elected representatives is not required) then individual consultation is essential. The need for a communicative dialogue cannot be over-emphasised.*

12. The staffing of the whole organisation will be examined for any vacancies which some of those selected for redundancy might be able to fill.

   Note: *It is essential that the possibility of alternative work, to save redundancies, is constantly examined and possibilities discussed with those whose jobs are at risk.*

13. If alternative work is found for an employee, confirmation of such alternative work should be given to the employee with an indication of the length of a trial period, during which notice for termination due to redundancy will be suspended.

   Note: *An employee who is made an offer of suitable alternative work and rejects it unreasonably (e.g. without trying it) may lose the right to a redundancy payment.*

14. The redundancy payment will be calculated in accordance with the state scheme, save that there will be a minimum payment equal to two weeks' pay, all years of service will count, there will be no upper maximum on a week's pay, and the amount will be increased by 50%.

Note: There is no obligation to enhance the payments laid down by the state but a number of employers do so.

15. For employees nearing retirement, any enhanced redundancy payment will be restricted to the amount of gross pay they would have received between the expiry of their notice period and their normal retirement date.

16. All redundant employees will have available the employer's outplacement service which will attempt to help employees to consider their options and to find alternative positions.

Terms

Immediately an employee knows they could or are to lose their job as a result of redundancy they tend to have two immediate questions:

a) how long do they have in service before they will be required to leave, and

b) how much will they be entitled to in compensation?

Since such data can be difficult to remember, particularly in what can be a somewhat traumatic interview, it is essential that full written details setting out all options and entitlements are given to those selected immediately that they are told, and that some named source of answers to the questions that may arise from time to time is provided. Clear honest information and communication can help defuse much of the antipathy that may otherwise be generated. Most people are quite capable of accepting and coping with bad news – even the loss of their jobs. What they resent is not being given full information or being treated as incapable of appreciating the reality of the situation. Statements about the situation should be given using straightforward honest English – trying to soften bad news – but note that the use of euphemisms and JARGON does not make the truth more palatable: it merely adds insult to injury. Counselling services can be useful in this situation, and may help individuals to come to terms with the loss of their job.

Outplacement

Increasingly organisations making employees redundant realise the moral obligation they have to such employees and attempt to provide facilities to help them find alternative jobs. If this can be refined and advertised then it should provide some reassurance to those affected that assistance is available. Outplacement can range from the provision of a written guide to seeking and interviewing for another job, to full career guidance, re-writing career histories and CVs and even head-hunting on behalf of those affected.

It should not be overlooked that there may be tasks the organisation will require to be done on a bought-in basis which might be sourced by redundant employees acting in a 'self-employed' capacity. Assistance given to redundant employees to start their own businesses may be not only well-received by those directly affected but provide a clear message to all concerned regarding the attitude of the company to its responsibilities.

Case study: Phoenix

During the running down of a business in Plymouth, several redundant employees were assisted in setting up their own businesses. Although their original employer ceased business, five years later three of the new businesses were still running. During the run-down record output was achieved, almost certainly reflecting the positive response of employees to the efforts being made by the then employer to source alternative jobs for them.

Aftermath

Inevitably the greatest attention needs to be given to those who are to lose their jobs. However, it should not be overlooked that those who remain also need as much as information as can be given to them. However, reassurance regarding future employment prospects, which will understandably concern many, should only be provided where it is completely safe to do so and if given should be limited to a set period. Providing unwarranted reassurance would be counter-productive since should it be proven to have been baseless the credibility of all associated with it will be lost. Those remaining often experience feelings of guilt that 'they' were not chosen to be made redundant and these feelings will need to be countered.

> Note: Basically the more thought that can be given to the problems in advance of the need for action, the more likely the organisation is to be able to deal productively with all the questions and difficulties that will be experienced. Trying to deal with such problems without time to consider all the ramifications, or more commonly trying to evade so dealing, is likely to lead to disastrous consequences.

Doasyouwouldbedoneby

Redundancy has been used as an example of bad news requiring to be communicated – not least since it occurs all too frequently nowadays. However, the principles of developing a policy/procedure in advance and of ensuring that it is adhered to at the time applies to all instances where bad news is to be communicated. The principle of 'doasyouwouldbedoneby' (from Charles Kingsley's *The Water Babies*) is perhaps a sound criteria. If the person who is responsible for undertaking the communication can picture themselves as the other party and tailor their comments, attitude and response as if they were the one receiving the bad news, this may help achieve an understanding of how the other party feels and is likely to respond. Attempting to see matters as the other party is likely to see them and to visualise their responses may be the first step to constructive communication in such circumstances. However, it sometimes happens that if the bad news is really totally unexpected, the recipient is unable to comprehend other information (even details of payments and benefits) for some time. This may be true even though it seems to the party breaking the news that the other person is absorbing what is being said. Their eyes may seem to be alert but vision and hearing may actually have switched off whilst the brain races to assimilate all the implications of the news. In redundancy the most common immediate reaction is panic at the thought of the ongoing bills and costs and how these will be faced without an income. In realisation of this some employers have made the announcement on a Friday, provided written data at that stage and invited employees to discuss the situation the following Monday, by which time they assume the realities of the situation may have sunk in and the employees may be more able to absorb information and ask meaningful questions. This is the whole rationale behind the legal obligation to consult employees in such a situation – most of us take time to generate a considered response.

There is a considerable danger that in not allowing time for absorption of the message, and giving the impression that there is little time or interest in the reaction, TEMPER will be generated – and there is little hope of any communication (i.e. joint understanding of the subject matter) when tempers are lost.

Briefing

Introduction

A MORI survey disclosed that in order of preference employees ranked 'face-to-face' communication with their immediate leader as their most preferred method of communication. Small briefings, large briefings and written communication were the next highest ranked methods. Realistically in a company of any size, other than in appraisal or MENTORING situations, it is virtually impossible for face-to-face communication to take place in the workplace on a regular basis. The more logical step is to arrange small-group briefings.

Title

In this respect the word 'briefing' is used to describe any meeting of up to (say) 40–50 employees coming together with their manager or a more senior manager to discuss work-related items. Such groups may be known as 'taskforces', 'updating sessions', 'team meetings', 'quality circles', and so on. The title is irrelevant, since the underlying purpose of each, to allow/generate communication on matters of interest to all involved, is virtually the same. Briefings fall into three main types:

- team meetings where the composition is only the team who normally work together (e.g. the Payroll Department) and the subject matter is their work and the problems directly related thereto
- cascade briefings where the audience is the work-team but the subject matter may comprise more general issues than their work-related items
- management briefings where employees from more than one department may be gathered together to be updated for a specific purpose, by a senior manager.

To a considerable extent all such devices can be termed 'investing in people' whilst not necessarily being related to the movement that bears that name. Formal rules are not required to be able to invest in people, although the Investors in People (IIP) initiative cannot be faulted. Quoted in the CBI's *Corporate Communicators' Handbook* (Kogan Page, 1997) are the following statistics from organisations introducing IIP:

- a chemist increased its operating margins from 7% to 11%
- a stationer saw a 41% increase in profits and a 40% reduction in labour turnover in two years
- a manufacturer saved 60% on purchases and improved customer spending by 200%
- a firm of solicitors improved their net profit by 45%
- a borough council reduced manpower by 13% whilst achieving higher service levels and
- a building group reduced accidents by 50%.

Team meetings

These are the most favoured types of briefings since the subjects discussed tend to be of direct interest to the employees – their own work and problems and difficulties related thereto. Since interface is with their immediate superior they are also less likely to be deterred from speaking out. In all kinds of briefing the input of the leader is essential, but this may be more of a challenge for leaders of team meetings since they may be supervisors untrained and inexperienced in giving PRESENTATIONS. To ensure effectiveness all those who will be expected to run such sessions should be given coaching whilst the guidance set out in the following checklist may also be of assistance.

Checklist: Team meeting – principles and practice

1. Monthly meeting led by the supervisor/manager attempting to be as informal as possible
2. Team leader needs to prepare by

   - listing problems for team consideration
   - considering suggestions made
   - arranging for a team member to take notes and to have these available at subsequent meetings
   - having available company briefing.

3. Team leader must ensure all questions raised are noted and answered either during the meeting or subsequently if the information is not immediately available. (Note that answers will be provided unless this would breach confidentiality, in which case this will be stated.)
4. Team leader should ensure sufficient time is allowed for discussion of items. Meetings will not normally last more than 30–45 minutes.

Team leader preparation

(a) Collect news from your own and other departments (arrange exchange with team leaders from linked departments)

(b) (If linked with cascade briefing – see below) familiarise yourself with the content of the company briefing, obtaining answers to anticipated questions

(c) Collect suggestions made from those in the team, consider objectively, list problems and advantages but do not pre-judge – let the team discuss and come to its own conclusion(s)

(d) Check that all questions raised at previous meeting have been answered and, if not, obtain/prepare answers for the team

(e) List all items for consideration in a checklist for reference during the meeting to ensure nothing is overlooked.

Running the meeting

(a) Three essentials – preparation, preparation, preparation!

(b) Remember that the meeting is purely a conversation such as you might have at the workplace. Try not to be nervous – it should be an informal chat with the aim of trying to understand each other's viewpoints, problems and aims.

(c) Forget about yourself – concentrate on the business you want to get through (from your checklist) and ensure team members have a fair hearing.

(d) Be enthusiastic – your attitude will motivate the team.

(e) Encourage all to participate. If certain members are shy or not forthcoming, try to involve them by asking whether they agree or disagree with items. Some employees will speak automatically but others may require encouragement. Help those who have difficulty expressing themselves by putting a version of what you think they are saying in your own words and then checking with them that you have it right.

(f) Stress that although the team welcomes the opportunity to deal with complaints, it is not just an opportunity for a grumble session. Suggest that anyone having a complaint should also be prepared to put forward a solution – the discussion can then be steered to the positive aspect of solution rather than the negative aspect of complaint.

(g) Don't imply that all problems have an immediate answer – or that the team should know all the answers. If there is a question without an answer, refer back to line management to try to find the answer and let the team know this at the next following meeting.

(h) Summarise the discussion and decisions before closing the meeting. Ensure any members who have been asked to carry out tasks know this.

(i) Set the date for the next briefing.

(j) If required to cancel the team briefing meeting: DON'T.

> *Note: If it is absolutely impossible to hold the briefing at the date/time stated, then postpone the meeting by no more than two working days, but never cancel even if there seems little to discuss.*

Cascade briefing

The principle of cascade briefing (advocated by the Industrial Society for many years) is that the people with the ultimate responsibility for generating employee communication are senior management. This is indisputable – albeit often overlooked. However, the idea of cascade briefing then goes on to suggest that senior management should brief middle management who should brief junior management who should brief supervision who should brief employees. Whilst this may be fine in principle it assumes that all those doing the briefing are committed to the principle, able and willing to brief adequately and to answer the questions that the briefing session will generate, and that there will be no barriers to the disclosure of information. This is unfortunately unlikely to be the case in some organisations.

Firstly there can be resistance from some managers to both the principle and practice, and this will need to be overcome. However, forcing someone to carry out a procedure will not necessarily ensure that it is carried out well or effectively. Secondly few people are natural communicators and messages can become distorted either because the speaker does not necessarily understand the matter fully or because he/she cannot deliver the message in a clear way (i.e. in terms capable of being understood by the audience). Finally where the subject matter is particularly complex and not fully understood by the briefer it is very unlikely that they will be able to answer questions which are an important part (in many respects an essential part) of the briefing process. Faced with questions they could either try to bluff their way out or admit ignorance and need to refer back. This the briefer may feel is a reflection on them, i.e. they may feel that having to say 'I don't know' undermines their authority.

In addition the messages can be misconstrued in repetition. The case study quoted in ARROGANCE recites the classic problem of a confident message emanating from the chief executive being translated and mangled in repetition until it reached the ears of the intended audience in a form almost exactly the opposite of that intended. Even with the utmost commitment to the truth it is difficult to repeat to someone else anything other than the simplest message in the way intended by the originator. This simple truth reflects the inherent danger of cascade briefing. However, it can be made even worse since delegating communication empowers those down the line with the opportunity should they wish to filter and skew the messages. In addition any feedback or return messages also run the risk of being mangled in repetition, if not similarly filtered.

If Number One cannot speak personally and widely (and consistently) to those at the sharp end then a message must be consigned to paper and distributed. Even then the words used should be examined carefully for unwanted undertones or misinterpretations. Simple language needs to be used: jargon or words not in everyday use can confuse and mar the effectiveness of the message.

Senior management involvement

Each of the problems highlighted above can be overcome by adequate training which itself underlines the necessity for any such procedure to be introduced only after all involved have received training in making presentations and dealing with questions outside their spheres of knowledge. This in turn, however, discloses another problem – that cascade briefing's greatest value (that of disseminating information to a large number of people in a short space of time by using the management chain of authority) is also its greatest weakness since the process will inevitably generate questions and there needs to be a 'reverse cascade' by which such questions can 'flow up' to the Board and answers can 'flow back'. Even where such a process is set up, some managers may 'filter out' questions which they feel may reflect badly on themselves or concern matters they do not want discussed. Setting up an effective 'reverse cascade' can pose so great a logistic problem that it may be preferable rather than using the cascade principle to appoint one senior manager to carry out all the briefings on a regular basis. This has a number of advantages:

- the quality of the various briefings is more likely to be even
- the briefings themselves may gain in prestige by being conducted by a senior manager or director
- by virtue of the manager's seniority they should have personal access to all information on which questions could be asked. This should allow them to answer most of the questions posed from their personal knowledge and, where they do not have the information, they can revert individually to the questioner(s).

Conversely the fact that the briefings are being conducted by a senior manager may stifle some contributions, and great care needs to be taken to preserve the authority of the intervening management.

The brief

Regardless of whether cascade or direct senior management briefings are being used (and even in some cases where team briefings are in operation) the process of dissemination of information can be aided by the preparation of a regular management brief giving salient facts to act as a record of what was discussed and as a spur to discussion.

Example: Management brief

Organisation   Briefing sheet ref. no. . . . .

Date prepared   Briefing to be completed by [date]

1. *Company position*
To [date of subject period] sales are . . . [up] on budget, profits are . . . [up] on budget.

2. *Orders*
The order book is satisfactory with . . . weeks' orders in house.

Special information (general news of particular orders, special interest, etc.)

3. *Promotional activity*
News of product developments, new launches reactions, advertising campaigns

4. *Production information*
Productive units achieved compared with budget, downtime, lost time, quality – achieved and problems. Anticipated demand in productive terms, etc.

5. *Personnel information*
System changes. New state requirements, etc.

6. Health and safety matters

7. Other general information

8. Contacts for further information/answers to questions raised at previous briefings

---

Carelines

Introduction

Aspects of dealing with customers is dealt with in CUSTOMER CARE, but one method whereby such complaints can be defused or dealt with before they arise is through the provision of a telephone 'careline'. The theory, which seems to be borne out in practice, is that if customers are provided with a telephone number and invited to voice their views on a variety of subjects, the main thrust of any antipathy they feel will be dissipated, rapport or understanding (on both sides) may be attained – and in addition feedback is obtained. The value of the careline system is thus not just that the ire of disaffected customers (who are often likely to tell well over 20 others of their dissatisfaction) may be dissipated, but also that it can be an inexpensive form of market research. It can provide a most valuable form of customer communication.

Administration

A careline requires a dedicated telephone number, manned at all times by a person of sufficient seniority, training and knowledge that they can

- deal competently with every enquiry
- make and implement decisions if necessary that may entail paying compensation or making rectification
- deal with each caller in a tactful, sympathetic yet firm manner without becoming flustered or annoyed despite what can be considerable antipathy and even anger.

Recent press reports indicate that customers are now more prepared to complain – and use the phone to do so. Advice for those manning such lines (whether dedicated carelines, or straightforward customer complaint lines) is

- own the conversation by providing a contact name immediately (the use of a first name may assist gaining a rapport)
- listen carefully rather than talking (talking can indicate dismissiveness to the caller.)

- make 'sympathetic' noises from time to time when the caller is speaking to demonstrate attentiveness and appreciation
- sound positive and interested (a lack of interest or implied boredom will merely aggravate the situation)
- summarise the complaint or suggestion to ensure it has been noted properly
- thank the caller for the call and, if a response is needed, make a promise to return the call (and then stick to that promise).

Purpose

Carelines can be used

- to allow customers to make comments and/or complaints about products or service thus providing a crude survey of customer reactions ('crude' since only those who feel strongly, one way or another, are likely to use the service)
- to allow members of the public to 'report' poor service (e.g. driving). This can be effected by displaying a careline number on organisation vehicles with an invitation to others to ring the number if they feel the driving of the organisation vehicle left something to be desired. In fact several of the organisations that operate such a system report that they have had very few calls – in the main they feel the fact that their own drivers know they can be reported acts as a spur to them to drive with consideration for other road users.
- to act as a means whereby the organisation can promote its products and carry out customer research on products, plans, etc.

Benefit

Whilst allowing customers to complain and/or make suggestions is valuable, if only since it can often draw the sting of the complaint and avoid (or allow inexpensive) restitution, those organisations using the system also record the benefit of being able to conduct market research with captive customers whose views on a whole range of matters related to the product and indeed to its competitors can be checked.

Case study: In use

(a) Mars Confectionery have operated carelines for some time and now receive a very large number of calls every hour. The tenor of most calls is very positive, although some callers do use the freephone number purely as a means of talking to another person whilst a tiny proportion take the opportunity of being abusive (a phenomenon noted by other careline providers – see below). Mars conduct a mini research survey on every caller and, by taking their personal details, also generate a mailing list of those who state that they like Mars products.

(b) BurgerKing, the fast food chain, wished to move away from a system whereby every customer letter had to be answered by letter. They encourage customers to use a careline by displaying its contact number not only in store, but even on the customer's till receipts. In dealing with the calls the company is able to derive considerable assistance in the development of its service and product range.

An investment

Carelines can be expensive to set up. For example, Nintendo, the computer games specialists, spend over £50,000 a year running their telephone helpline. This service was actually intended to provide assistance to Nintendo game-users, rather than deal with general product queries and complaints. However, it is possible that the provision of the helpline may have prevented some customers from relieving their frustration by ceasing to buy Nintendo products. If so the expenditure of £50,000 (itself tiny compared to the cost of advertising their products) pales into insignificance.

Yet the head of a company providing such a service commented in a *Sunday Times* interview 'The single most important factor preventing the spread of carelines in the UK is a lack of appreciation by senior managers of the importance of providing answers to customer queries.' Yet surely there can be few endeavours more important to the continuation of the organisation than dealing with and listening to its customers. Unless an organisation listens to its customers it is likely to lose them, as its perception of what they want could swiftly become out of date. Leading consultants Price Waterhouse discovered in a survey of the top 200 UK companies that losing existing customers costs British industry around £100 billion each year – which coincidentally is about the same amount spent on marketing and sales helping to replace such lost sales.

In the UK only 22% of consumer goods producers use careline numbers, whereas in the USA 83% of consumer goods (including all household goods) carry careline numbers.

Devotees of the careline type of service suggest that if consumers who complain are dealt with swiftly and professionally (particularly on a freephone number) then it is almost certain they will become regular customers – rather than angry ex-customers, and it is far less costly to service existing customers than to source replacements.

Case study: The real thing

Coca-Cola put a freephone telephone number on its soft drinks packaging and receives an average of just under 3000 calls per week which raise all sorts of points, although only around 10% are complaints. The company believes that its careline acts as a very good filter to indicate if there are going to be widespread problems – with which it can then deal – as well as being a very good way of gauging interest in new products. When the company had problems with a sales promotion advertisement on the products the number of calls rose sharply.

When Coca-Cola introduced 'New Coke' its careline was inundated with complaints from its customers. To the company's credit it responded immediately and reinstated the previous recipe. Had the Careline not existed no outlet would have been provided for these comments, sales would have dropped alarmingly possibly without the company knowing why – at least immediately.

Footnote: The New Coke experience should be a salutary lesson for those who believe implicitly in market research. After all the acceptability of the new recipe had been extensively researched yet it was only the Careline that provided the real thing.

Backlash

The use of a careline can, however, encourage calls of which a proportion will be hoax, useless, or even insulting and vicious. Counselling and training needs to be given to staff to try to help them cope with these kinds of calls. The response to calls which are abusive should be that the call is being tape-recorded and the number traced. This is relatively easy now via the use of the 1471 number, remembering that details of the calls are available to the police even if the caller has previously blocked recovery of the number using the alternative code.

Where threats or foul language are used the caller should be advised that they are committing an offence and details may be passed to the police for investigation. Under the Telecommunications Act (1984) 'a person who by means of a public communication system, sends a message or other matter that is . . . menacing, or . . . causes annoyance . . .' is guilty of an offence and can be fined on conviction.

Communication policy

Introduction

One effective way to ensure there is adequate information provided for (and hopefully generating communication with) all interested parties is by the application of the requirements of a communication policy stating who needs what and with what regularity. The policy provides a foundation, as well as a criteria, on which can be built a number of initiatives to ensure good communication and, in overall terms, the achievement of the AIMS of the business.

Definition

A communication policy can be defined as a statement made and disseminated by the business by which it commits itself to the regular production and distribution of information and/or allows two-way transference of information, creating communicative opportunities. For each initiative and target audience it needs to incorporate a statement of intent followed by details of the methods by which the intent can be implemented.

Execution

In the following examples the needs and methods of informing the employees and shareholders of an organisation are addressed. Similar policies would need to be generated covering COMMUNITY RELATIONS as well as relationships with suppliers and the media.

Example: Personnel communication policy

Statement of Intent: The organisation wishes to involve all personnel in its activities, to encourage their active participation in its progress, including decision-making, and to benefit by their comments and ideas. It commits itself to the regular dissemination of information and to the encouragement of inter-organisation and interpersonnel communication which is to encompass personal as well as organisational activities.

Execution:

1. On appointment each employee will be given a wallet containing
   - (a) contract of employment
   - (b) employee handbook
   - (c) health, safety, training and fire precautions statements
   - (d) copy of latest employee report
   - (e) copy of latest newsletter (group)
   - (f) copy of any divisional/site publication.

2. During employment employees will receive
   - (a) Annual/employee report (annually)
   - (b) Interim results (annually)
   - (c) Newsletter (quarterly/monthly/fortnightly, etc.)
   - (d) Local divisional newsletter or equivalent
   - (e) Regular management-organised and -run briefing sessions
   - (f) *Ad hoc* briefing sessions as required
   - (g) Representation at Works Council/Joint Consultative meeting
   - (h) Copies of Council/Committee minutes
   - (i) Representation on Safety/Redundancy/other Committee
   - (j) Copies of Safety/Redundancy/other Committee minutes

General commitment:

Management is expected and encouraged to keep employees informed of all activities and developments in an informal manner, there being no substitute for such face-to-face communication. Regular team briefings will take place, in which forum all employees are encouraged to participate. In addition senior management will run at least two briefing sessions each year – primarily to deal with questions arising from the publication of the organisation's interim and final results.

Managers are expected:

(a) to spend a large proportion of their time with the employees who comprise their teams, and

(b) when in their office to operate an open-door policy.

Employees are encouraged to take a lively interest in the activities of the company and, if there is anything on which they have insufficient information or about which they are unsure, they should be encouraged to ask their immediate superiors, and, should they not receive an adequate answer, to pursue their query through the grievance procedure set out in the company handbook.

Example: Shareholder communication policy

Statement of Intent: The company wishes to involve all shareholders in its activities and to encourage their participation in its progress, recognising that most shareholders could also be customers and it is in everyone's interests if sales generating an adequate return are buoyant.

The company commits itself to the regular dissemination of information to its shareholders by means of user-friendly interim and preliminary statements and annual reports. Recognising that not all shareholders will wish to receive the full report it will make available a user-friendly Summary Financial Statement and will also send to every shareholder a copy of the report produced for all employees.

Execution:

1. When a shareholder invests in the company they will be sent a letter of welcome individually signed by the Chairman together with copies of the latest annual and employee reports and details of the financial calendar.

2. Every shareholder will also be invited to be placed on the mailing list to receive the employee newsletter.

3. Although details of the Preliminary Announcement will be published in national newspapers, each shareholder will be sent an individual copy.

4. With each Annual Report and Notice of Annual General Meeting shareholders will be sent a full 'plain English' version of every resolution to be considered at the meeting. (Similar explanatory letters will be generated and sent should it be necessary to convene Extraordinary General Meetings.)

5. All shareholders will be encouraged to attend meetings of the company and to make their views known, or to submit proxies if unable to attend.

6. At every meeting of the company, members of the Board will be available to meet shareholders individually for 30 minutes before the meeting and for a similar time afterwards, so that individual questions, etc., can be dealt with, the restrictions of Insider-dealing regulations permitting.

7. Shareholders holding [number] shares or more will be entitled to apply for the shareholder discount card allowing them to obtain a discount from the company's [goods, shops, services, etc.] up to a maximum value for each year of [amount].

8. Details of shareholder days will be provided at the start of each financial year and shareholders will be encouraged to visit the company's premises on those days. Each location will arrange suitable tours with refreshments and for a director to be available to answer questions (Insider-dealing regulations permitting).

9. At and around the time of the Annual General Meeting a shareholder CARELINE (its number having been advertised in the Annual Report) will be manned by a director to answer questions and queries (Insider-dealing regulations permitting) from those shareholders unable to attend the meeting.

Community relations

Introduction

Organisations operate within societies, and most recognise that since without such infrastructure they could not operate there is an obligation (as well as increasing pressure) for organisations to contribute to society. This is particularly important where the activities of the organisation could be damaging to the environment. To create an impression of itself within the community, the organisation needs to communicate effectively with the community, not least since local and central authorities have powers through which they can control – even curtail – aspects of the activities of commercial organisations.

Commitment

The link with community and communal obligations is all-pervading. For example – most commercial organisations are already subject to planning considerations (including increasingly stringent fire precautions) requiring them to conform with area plans. Attempting to develop a site whilst ignoring such requirements could be very expensive since powers exist that may require an organisation to demolish unapproved building and to reinstate anything removed. A commitment to a policy such as is set out in the following checklist may be helpful.

Checklist: Community relationship

1. The organisation commits itself as a responsible member of society to treat the general public, the community and its local and national authorities and the environment within which it operates with respect.
2. At all times the organisation will act in accordance with all requirements placed upon it by central and local government and statutory authorities and expects all employees to adhere to the same principle.

3. The organisation will continue to be a member of the Business in the Community movement, and will support other local initiatives, encouraging its employees to join in schemes aimed at enhancing the environment within which we operate, by means of day and block release or secondment, and encourages the communication of the results of such work to other employees.

4. The organisation recognises the importance of environmental issues and commits itself to work towards the introduction of processes and practices that least harm, or do not harm at all, the environment. It welcomes ideas for protecting the environment from its operations from whatever source, and will work to introducing such feasible and viable ideas – including allowing flexibility of working hours to enable employees to share transport to and from home.

5. The organisation will work towards the reduction/elimination of waste and the maximisation of the use of resources.

6. The views of pressure groups and those representing environmental groups will be considered objectively and borne in mind when making decision on these issues.

7. The organisation will endeavour to support local education establishments generally, and in detail by (for example) encouraging employees to be governors of schools, sponsoring projects undertaken by local schools, etc.

8. Official agencies demanding access will be dealt with courteously and in accordance with the access policy which determines to what information such persons may have access.

9. The organisation will occupy and use its facilities with due regard for the interests of its neighbours whether these be domestic or business.

10. The organisation will always take part in and support local community projects (whether these be of a security, fund-raising or any other type) except projects which have a political bias.

11. Complaints about the activities of the organisation will be dealt with courteously and with patience. A full investigation will be mounted, the findings will be conveyed to the complainant and a record kept by [name].

12. Wherever possible waste product will be saved for recycling either internally or externally. The organisation will provide suitable facilities for this purpose and encourages all employees to use its facilities to recycle waste products from their own homes and undertakings. Any income derived from such recycling activities will be donated to educational or charitable causes.

Conferences (press, sales, etc.) and exhibitions

Introduction

Conferences are held for a variety of purposes; however, they all have similar requirements, albeit with particular variations. Despite the ever-increasing range of opportunities for communicating over distance (i.e. by remaining in our office or home and communicating with others electronically) there seems to be an ever-increasing demand for conference, seminar, etc., facilities – perhaps because, man being a gregarious animal, most people do still prefer to meet face to face. The best-produced internet WEB SITE, the glossiest brochure, the most informative e-mail cannot compare with a well-produced and delivered interactive PRESENTATION. Even video-conferencing lacks immediacy, since only the views and sounds captured by the camera are transmitted.

Preparation

Any event which places the organisation in the public eye needs to be carefully planned. In addition, rather like the difference between cinema and the theatre, the fact that there is a live interface poses an added dimension for those responsible. Literally we may only have 'one chance to get it right' – there can be no rehearsal if there is a live interface – our rehearsing needs to be done before we go live. The questions in the following checklist could form a basis for discussion.

Checklist: Preparing for an event

1. Define the exact purpose of the event – what are we trying to achieve?
2. Determine if there any potential negative effects and, if so, consider whether these can be neutralised or need to be addressed as part of the event or in some other way.
3. Define the target audience and their interests.
4. Ensure that the target audience is addressed within the promotional material.

5. Present material and related aspects of the events in a way that will satisfy the interests of the target audience.

6. Determine and prepare the location of the event with particular relevance to

- suitability for the type of event,
- convenience primarily for the target audience but also for those involved in presenting,
- comfort and accessibility, for all involved, particularly should those with disabilities be expected to attend) and
- transport facilities for all involved. Is there suitable public services or adequate car parking and/or shuttle transport, etc.

Note: *The growth in provision of conference, etc., facilities is referred to above. Obviously the investment this requires is generated by a belief of a growth in demand. Facilities which are entirely suitable may be rare and thus in demand – hence bookings of the ideal site may need to be made early.*

7. Prepare all paperwork from the viewpoint of the reader. This is particularly important for prospective customers and media representatives (see PRESS RELEASE) but the same principle should apply to all those presented with written information.

8. Ensure all aspects of the presentation are addressed so that the overall appearance is in accord with the required style, message, and intent of the organisation and of the event.

Case study: Detailed approach

When the famous loose-leaf diary company Filofax was floated as a public company, the directors each had their presentation notes in a Filofax binder. In this way not only was the presence of the product much to the fore when the future of the company was being determined but also the versatility of the six- and nine-ring binders then being developed by the company was demonstrated. Literally members of the press could see the product in use in front of them. Similarly the placing document was reproduced and given to all present in a six-ring binder.

---

9. Check everything for accuracy. Whilst this should be stating the obvious there are instances where inaccuracies have not been eradicated from material which obviously does not reflect well on the organisation – particularly if it is involved in products or services which themselves need to be exact, etc.

10. All those involved need to be briefed in what they are required to say, especially in dealing with difficult questions and people. If possible, answers should be rehearsed.

Press conferences

As set out in the comments on PRESS RELEASE, the first consideration should be to ensure that the news is really newsworthy. It may be of considerable interest to the organisation but only of superficial interest to anyone else. In many ways, however, this is even more important with a conference than a release. The printed page can simply be ignored and 'spiked' with other stories which 'didn't make it', but should a reporter have attended a conference in the expectation of a newsworthy story only to find that there is no substance, it could spark a negative report immediately or later.

Assuming there really is a story to be told then a presenter needs to be nominated and coached in dealing not just with making the PRESENTATION but also with fielding difficult questions in a positive and polished way. The presenter is literally the public face of the organisation. The brief itself could comprise the story and its effect, plus if necessary (if only to pre-empt questions)

* background (financial results, position in market, etc.), and
* other challenges and the organisation's approach to these.

In addition the presenter needs to be aware of any 'bad news' items concerned with the organisation, since the opportunity may be taken by those present to probe regarding such matters.

The timing of the conference is key to its success. If the subject is something that will be of interest to (say) Sunday paper browsers then there is little point announcing it on a Monday. Conversely if it is something where national daily coverage is required there may be little point releasing it on a Friday since readers' attention to news in Saturday papers is less than other weekdays. Conversely if the subject is such that it could form the basis for a feature article, timing it for inclusion in Saturday's paper may be advantageous. If television attention is sought it should be remembered that this could mean the story gaining coverage far faster than other audiences using different channels of communication.

Sales conferences

Normally these are used as 'selling opportunities' to outsiders (agents, franchise-holders, customers) or 'morale-boosting' events to internal staff (which could also include agents). The temptation to oversell is high but better avoided. 'Hyping' the organisation should fool few people and may annoy those who recognise the 'hype' for what it is. However, a certain amount of encouragement is obviously necessary and this could include the following subjects:

- a résumé of progress, targets achieved or missed, etc.
- a realistic analysis of competition and market demand
- details of new products, pricing changes, etc., and why these are better than the competition (or reasons why they are not – since it is better for those attempting to sell the product to know its shortcomings and be prepared to overcome objections based on these than to be taken unawares)
- details of any changes to commission or wages
- incentives, prizes, etc. – the point being to try to end on an upbeat note.

Above all what is essential is not just feedback from the audience, but also encouragement to everyone to make suggestions, comments, etc. Only by allowing this will the binding together of the team be likely to be achieved.

Exhibitions

In this area, since very often the target audience tends to be customers or at least potential customers, the possibility of 'hype' is more acute. Those on 'the stand' should certainly take opportunities to 'sell' their organisation and its products, but in view of legislation in this field overselling or exaggerating the performance or capacity of the products should be avoided. Better to have a factual résumé backed with figures, examples or samples, video and other demonstrations. To some extent those manning the stand will sell the organisation and its products or services by selling themselves. Accordingly they need to be completely briefed, not just on all aspects of the products or services, etc., but also on the organisation itself, its aims and commitments. During the event they will *be* the organisation. Care should be taken to ensure there is an adequate number of representatives manning the stand, so that breaks can be taken, thereby keeping everyone fresh. Conversely there should not be so many of the 'home team' on the stand that customers and/or others are inhibited from attending.

Events

Sponsoring sporting events is one way of promoting the organisation's name – albeit often an expensive one. Few organisations have the time or experience to organise this themselves and it may be preferable to commission professionals to make the arrangements. If so, references should be taken up on the proposed body to check what they provide and the quality of their service. Consideration should also be given, if the event is open-air (e.g. a horse race) to arranging alternatives should the weather be inclement. Whilst guests may be disappointed that the function itself could not run, they may not fail to be impressed that, at what may be seem to be very short notice, the organisation has been able to arrange alternative entertainment for them. An organisation which can consider such an eventuality and arrange it at short notice should in this way enhance its reputation – which presumably was the point of running the event in the first place.

Consultation channels

Introduction

Many activities featured here are a matter of good practice, and organisations have the choice whether to accept and implement or to ignore them. Increasingly, however, employers are legally required to communicate with (i.e. consult) their employees in certain circumstances. In doing so the various techniques set out in this book can be used to engender good-quality communication which will be essential in these instances. Tribunals are on record stressing that consultation must be realistic – i.e. it must enable employees to have input and for their views to be taken into account rather than merely noted.

Trade union activities

Employers have been obliged to consult with trade unions recognised for collective bargaining as a result of earlier legislation which was consolidated in the Trade Union and Labour Relations (Consolidation) Act (1992). However, such requirements (sometimes enhanced) are normally set out in a local or national union agreement.

In addition to the general requirement to consult a recognised trade union, an employer is also required to provide such information that is necessary for the trade union to conduct collective bargaining. This could include financial information so that the effect of claims could be gauged.

Redundancy

Under the Collective Redundancies and Transfer of Undertakings (Protection of Employment) (Amendment) Regulations (1995), employers who seek to make 20 or more employees redundant within a period of 90 days are required to consult with elected representatives of the employees likely to be affected 'in good time'. The representatives need not be union representatives, even though these may be available, as long as they are employees who are elected by their colleagues. If there are no elected representatives then the onus is on the employer to arrange for elections.

The consultation itself must be real – i.e. the employees' representatives must not be presented with a *fait accompli,* but their views and suggestions must be sought and taken into consideration. Failure to comply with this requirement could render any dismissals for redundancy to be unfair.

'In good time' is the somewhat imprecise phrase used in the legislation. Consultation must begin at least 30 days before the first dismissal and, if there are 100 or more redundancies to be effected, at least 90 days before the first occurs.

In engendering consultation an employer should disclose

- the reasons for the situation and suggestion of redundancy
- the numbers required to be made redundant and the total number at the establishment(s) affected
- any proposed method of selection, timing, etc.
- the method of calculating redundancy pay.

> *Note:* *This requirement is in addition to the requirement to consult meaningfully with those made redundant in all cases – that is even where fewer than 20 are being made redundant. It is thus good practice, having consulted in general terms and determined the basis for selection, to then consult on an individual basis. Consultation should be undertaken on an individual basis concerning all the above items and any alternative work where general consultation is not required.*

Transfer of undertaking

Where an undertaking is sold to a new owner both transferer and transferee have an obligation to 'inform the representatives of their respective employees affected by the transfer' of

- the reasons for the transfer and its suggested date
- legal, economic and social implications and,
- in relation to the employees, all measures envisaged.

Like the requirement set out above in relation to redundancy, the consultation must begin 'in good time' before the transfer takes place. If measures envisaged are contemplated then the consultation is required 'with a view to seeking agreement'.

'Employees affected' is another phrase which may be regarded as somewhat imprecise. It is intended to cover 'any employees who may be affected by the transfer or by measures taken in connection with it' – a definition which is extremely wide. Consultation must take place regardless of the numbers involved – there is no minimum.

Safety

Under the Health and Safety at Work [etc.] Act (1974) employers are required to consult with safety representatives appointed by recognised trade unions. The appointment of such representatives is dealt with in the Safety Representatives and Safety Committee Regulations (1977) which state that consultation 'in good time' should take place

- on the introduction of any measure (including new technologies) at the workplace which has health and safety implications for the workforce
- to provide health and safety information to employees
- to provide the planning and organisation of health and safety training
- to consider the employer's arrangements for appointing or nominating 'competent persons' to assist in safety matters (as required under the Management of Health and Safety at Work Regulations (1992).

> *Note:* *Under the Health and Safety (Consultation with Employees) Regulations (1996), employers are required to consult with employees or the representatives of all employees (not simply trade union members) on matters of health and safety.*

In addition (under section 100 of the Employment Rights Act, 1996) employers have an implied obligation to listen to any employee who has a reasonable concern for his safety or the safety of others.

Pensions

Under the Pensions Act 1995, unless their employer has obtained their permission to operate under alternative arrangements, members (including retired members) have the right to nominate at least one-third of the Trustees, who will have the same rights to information, etc. as other Trustees.

Discipline and dismissal

Although there is no specific requirement to consult with an employee when being disciplined or prior to his/her dismissal, it may be difficult to defend a claim of unfair dismissal if there has been no prior warning or discussion with an employee. Although it should be obvious that this is particularly true where the employee is being dismissed for lack of capability, even where there has been gross misconduct leading to what is normally referred to as 'instant dismissal', an employee should be given an opportunity to explain him/herself.

Disability

Although there is no specific requirement to consult with an employee, given that the employer is under an obligation under the Disability Discrimination Act 1995 to make 'reasonable adjustments' to the workplace to cater for an employee's disability, it is difficult to see how an employer could make a decision regarding the adjustment(s) needed unless consultation with the disabled person had taken place. Indeed the fact that such consultation had not taken place could be very damaging should the case be taken to a Tribunal. When attempting communication regarding compliance with the Act, employers are expected to have taken advice from suitable authorities on the subject. Thus communication with the subject is insufficient and there might need to be evidence that discussions had taken place with experts (e.g. in case of the employment of the deaf, hearing specialists, those providing lip-reading services and training, etc.).

Works Councils

Under the Maastricht Treaty the UK opted out of the EC Social Chapter which allowed it (*inter alia*) to avoid being bound by the requirements of the EC directive on Works Councils which applies to all organisations which have 1000 employees or more with the EC and at least two undertakings in different member states which each have at least 150 employees. The current UK Government has announced it will adopt the Social Chapter although it is believed it could take until 1999 for this to take place. When this occurs representatives to an organisation's Works Council will need to be elected and then the Council itself will have to be consulted on a range of topics which must be set out in domestic legislation.

The future

Once the UK opts in to the Works Council directive it is not impossible to imagine a situation where required consultation, currently fragmented and arising from a variety of sources, is re-examined and brought together as a responsibility of an employer's Works Council particularly as in summer 1997 there was a further proposal to reduce the minimum number of employees to 50, above which an employer would need to arrange for there to be a Works Council.

Corporate style

Introduction

The society within which modern day commercial organisations operate, increasingly demands that it be informed on all aspects of the operation. Such is the level of interest in their activities that some will find it intrusive – even running counter to the aims of the organisation which may require a certain degree of confidentiality. Generally, however, if the process by which the communication is managed is effective it should be capable of being manipulated to the organisation's benefit.

What is required is not only guidelines to determine how this communicative process can operate but also the style of the approach.

The overall approach

The sections in this book that relate to detailed approaches provide instant guidance to the person at the sharp end of the problem. Behind them is the general commitment of the organisation which may be reflected in its AIMS or within the COMMUNICATION POLICY. In addition we need a declaration of what we could call its corporate style – 'what we are about and how we go about it' or as former President George Bush once called it 'this vision thing'. This could be helpful not only in providing guidelines to all required to operate in the area but should also reinforce the rule that those involved in advertising, in public relations and in corporate design must operate within – indeed at all times reflect – the aegis of the corporate-style philosophy which to a large extent is itself a reflection of the reputation of the organisation. Reputations can take years to build and yet be lost in a few minutes by means of a few ill-considered words.

Case study: One four-letter word

Perhaps the best known incident which almost destroyed an organisation was Gerald Ratner's reference to some of the products that his shops sold as 'crap'. The remark from the chairman who had successfully built up one of the UK's largest chains of jewellers was intended humorously but the damage was immense. Ratner had to resign the chairmanship and eventually as a director, the share price plunged from 192p to 8p, around 200 shops in the chain were sold and the name of the remainder and the company was changed.

At all times the public face of the organisation whether in speech, printed or electronic word, quality of product or service, etc., should reflect (and indeed seek to enhance) the reputation of the organisation and all those connected should be aware that this is the aim – and their aim at all times: literally the task of addressing the stakeholders of the organisation is a responsibility of all managers at all times.

The public 'face' of the organisation needs to reflect reality – neither implying the organisation is better than it is (one wonders whether following two strikes which inconvenienced a considerable number of customers in 1996 and 1997, British Airways can really claim to be the 'world's favourite airline') nor hindering it by not reflecting its true value (as Gerald Ratner did). This is a concept only the Board can control – but is one that must be controlled at all times.

Failure to require that everyone seeks to maintain reputation or adheres to corporate style may lead to a situation where employees who need to represent the organisation externally in the course of their work have to operate by devising their own guidelines and style guide. This can only lead to inconsistencies and mean that decisions related to the appearance and promotion of the entity are not being taken in a cohesive and considered way, but rather executed in a piecemeal and fragmented manner not at all reflective of the way the organisation sees itself and wishes others to see it.

Checklist: Corporate style guidelines

1. The organisation as a responsible operator and employer will endeavour to communicate to all interested parties those details regarding its activities which may be of interest to them.
2. The areas of information that will be constantly reported upon are – future plans, new products (once any confidential aspects are removed), our competitive position, details regarding employment and benefits and our social responsibility programme.
3. Information will be provided, usually in written form under the authority of a [director] to ensure compliance with these guidelines.
4. This organisation has built a reputation for [honest dealing, good value products, quality service and responsible employment] over the years and wishes these characteristics to guide all connected with it in their

work and their relationships with external audiences at all times. No exceptions to these guidelines are acceptable. Failure to adhere to these precepts will be regarded very seriously.

5. Interviews can be granted with advance notice and an indication of the range of topics likely to be covered. Those interviewed will be required to comment only on items indicated in advance as being the subject matter. If questions outside this area are posed, the spokesperson will be required to answer 'policy requires that I do not answer questions on those subjects since I have not been briefed upon them'. Directors asked such questions may comment in general terms without committing the organisation.

6. All newsworthy information about the organisation will be published in press releases, and in all cases a contact will be provided so that additional information can be obtained.

The style of the approach

Ideally every item issued by an organisation should be presented in a common style reflective of its status or reputation. To achieve this means that the organisation needs to develop its own style guide or to adopt one already in existence. In 1993 the *Financial Times* published its own *Style Guide* (*Financial Times* Books). In 200 pages of user-friendly text a variety of guides are set out, plus examples of both good and acceptable as well as bad and rejected examples of written English. It is a sound and exhaustive guide, although other than the fact that it already exists and it saves reinventing the wheel, there is no reason why any organisation should use this particular guide rather than devising its own. The value of having a guide is that those required to write and pronounce will have a criteria that they know is acceptable to the directing body. In turn, the directing body will have rules with which they will expect all required to act to comply. Variances from the style guide can be challenged and the overall consistency thereby maintained.

Letterheads, etc.

If consistency of appearance is considered important then there need to be strict rules regarding the reproduction of the organisation name and logo on letterheads, invoices, adverts, premises, packaging, etc. The font used, as well as the size, colour and appearance, will all need to be determined. Legal requirements will also need to be taken into account. The rapid development of electronic communication and the informality of approach that tends to accompany this process have led to some company communications being issued which totally fail to adhere to previous standards and the legal requirements.

WARNING: Companies are required to include their registered office address, number and country of registration on their letterheads, etc. It is at least arguable that all such details should appear on correspondence using the e-mail system on the internet, since whilst the letter may not exist other than in electronic form, it is nevertheless an official communication from the company. This may be even more relevant when orders are being placed either automatically or on a one-off basis by electronic means.

Logos and emblems

Criticism is sometimes levelled at large organisations which spend what seem to be vast sums generating a logo or new logo. Yet a logo in many respects is one of the simplest yet most effective means of communicating the organisation, and giving an impression of what it is about, to the audience. It is the one entity that can without any words or description immediately conjure in the mind's eye of the viewer the style, rationale, products and approach of the organisation. A logo is both identification and advert, and in that context any investment should soon be repaid, although quantifying such investment will almost certainly be impossible. In a 1995 survey across 7000 people in the UK, USA, India, Japan and Australia, Sponsorship Research International discovered that the logos of the Olympic movement, McDonald's Restaurants, Shell Petrol and Mercedes cars were all recognised ahead of the symbol for Christianity – the cross.

Examples

(a) The impact of a recognisable logo should not therefore be under estimated. When Sir John Egan stipulated that the leaping jaguar – a symbol both of power and assertive prestige – should be reinstated on the bonnet of the Jaguar car, it immediately led to a considerable improvement in the attitude of those involved in the company. The emblem created a sense of pride in both product and organisation.

(b) BT (British Telecommunications) was criticised for spending £80 million to create and roll out through the company its (then new) stylised 'pipe player'. The cost was insignificant compared to the company's massive turnover, but the 'piper' creates a modern image of major player in the communications industry – which was not the case with its previous logo.

Note: Human nature is a strange beast. Whilst we tend to be creatures of habit we also like 'something new'. The sales of most products which fail to be updated periodically will fall – we will regard them as 'old-fashioned'. Similar attitudes can be evinced of organisations that fail to maintain a 'modern' image.

Footnote: McDonald's fought a libel case concerning their products in 1997. The dispute lasted over two years and received considerable publicity, not so much for the complained-of words but because the two people who ultimately were found to have libelled McDonald's defended themselves personally – even fighting the case to the High Court. McDonald's won the case but received only a small award with little chance of recovering their costs. Whilst the importance of challenging unfair criticism is undoubted there needs to be an assessment of the potential adverse publicity that could be generated by arguing too fiercely and being seen, as in this case, to be Goliath defeating a very small David. Here it seemed that 'even if you win, you lose'.

Crisis communication

Introduction

Most information or communication processes and procedures within the average organisation tends to be generated and used on a regular basis. Indeed only if objective information is available in this way will the process have credence and is it likely to supplant the 'grapevine' that exists in most organisations – and to enhance the reputation of the organisation. However, at times there will be a need for instant communication – often as a reaction to bad news. Since it is almost inevitable that at some time in the life of an organisation a disaster or adverse incident will occur it is advisable to prepare in advance since when a reaction is needed there may be little time available for planning – all time being needed to cope with the crisis.

Preparation

Crises tend to command two truisms

- they are unexpected, and
- they occur at the worst time.

In view of this there is a strong argument for trying to identify the implications of a range of crises and to consider what the communication requirements of each is likely to be and how they should be managed: see checklist.

Checklist: Crisis management

1. *Plan ahead*
   The range of disasters is considerable. Ideally there should be a plan for each eventuality. Such contingency planning lies outside the scope of this book. Here we are concerned with only the communication requirements of the crises.
2. *Be flexible*
   In managing a crisis flexibility, imagination and perception are essential. Management needs to be aware of the public dimension of potential problems.

Case study: A bad smell

In the same week that 2000 redundancies were announced one of the UK's largest companies declared that its Chief Executive was to receive a 40% pay increase. Both decisions may have been entirely justified and correct – but their juxtaposition seemed to indicate corporate ARROGANCE and called into question the managerial expertise of the company. Did those involved in these decisions not pause for one moment to imagine the outcry that would greet the announcements – and, if not, why not? The control of information and the public perspective of the organisation is part of management's role – i.e. seeking to avoid crises as well as deal with them, and certainly not to create them.

---

3. *List target audiences and their requirements*

    The essential questions that need to be asked (preferably in advance) are 'Given that we have to deal with X, who is it who will be affected immediately and later? Who of those then identified will we need to inform and how often will we need to keep them updated regarding progress? How, if we have two pieces of news which taken together reflect badly on us, can we manage the situation and minimise the danger?

4. *Dissemination*

    What means will we use to provide the information? Inevitably this will depend on the target audience and their requirements.

5. *Prepare the ground*

    This is particularly relevant to media reporters. If they are involved with the organisation for the first time, their deadlines will make it extremely unlikely that they will have time to go through a learning curve finding out what the organisation does (and does not) and the nature, role and attitude of those involved. As a result reports may well be based on impressions and conjecture rather than fact. Unfortunately, once published, these impressions tend to last in the minds of the audience receiving them, who can then take a great deal of convincing that an alternative version is true. Organisations whose existence, situation, products, etc. have a public profile should therefore consider making details available regularly so that a file of information, or simply informed personal knowledge, is available to be drawn upon in the event of a disaster. This may enable more accurate (even empathetic) reports to be generated. Waiting until there is a problem before trying to cultivate relations with and provide a background of information for the media (the so-called 'sticking-plaster' tactic of PUBLIC RELATIONS) is unlikely to be very successful even if the organisation is powerful.

6. *Obtain accurate information and tell the truth*
    Whoever is to be the spokesperson needs to be briefed and updated on the situation so that authoritative statements can be issued based upon the most recent information – and what is provided should be true. This may mean withholding information that the organisation would not wish to become public knowledge and then needing to answer 'no comment' to subsequent questions. Whilst this may lead to conjecture and speculation this may well be preferable to being caught out in a lie.

7. *Use ordinary language whatever the complexity*
    In *Tough Telephoning* (David Martin, Pitman, 1996) JARGON is defined as the refuge of the insecure, the device of the lazy and the response of the patronising. Further, in seeking to inform, one should never overestimate knowledge and never underestimate intelligence. If the originator of the message considers the target audience and prepares the content in a form that the target can understand, the most complex subject is capable of being transmitted and, more importantly, understood. The trick is in having enough time, inclination and perseverance to prepare the content accordingly. Time is likely to be at a premium in the aftermath of a disaster and thus it may be advisable to have already prepared plain English definitions of any processes, etc., which are complex. Using jargon, particularly in live interviews, can irritate both reporter and audience resulting in a backlash which could have been averted – and is certainly one of the last things one wants when there is a crisis. Conversely the fact that an obviously complex situation has been explained in plain English could help generate audience-rapport. Obviously such explanations need also to avoid any suspicion that the audience is being patronised.

Nature of the crisis

Crises tend to result from two main causes – external forces (particularly nature exercising its power) over which the organisation may have no control, and internal failures. In the former case those involved and the general public may have some sympathy for the organisation provided it shows that it can cope reasonably well with the aftermath. Conversely, in the case of the latter such goodwill may be absent from the outset and the organisation starts from a negative position – as did the organisation that instead of being flexible and cancelling a cruise, allowed one of its flagships to depart across the Atlantic whilst a refit of the ship was incomplete, and indeed with many of the refitter's employees still completing their work.

Obviously cancelling the cruise would have cost the company a considerable amount in compensation and would have attracted comments and adverse publicity, but it would have only been a fraction of the compensation it had to pay, and would probably have caused it to suffer only a fraction of the media attention it received when the full story broke. The poor management decision which allowed the ship to sail in such a state simply compounded the problem and turned a drama into the proverbial crisis.

Example

How much better would it have been to have contacted all the passengers a few days before the cancellation, offering (for example) full refund of the amount they had paid plus free tickets on a replacement cruise plus some monetary compensation, and then to have issued a press release announcing that the refit had been delayed and that the organisation had taken those steps. Everyone knows that problems occur – being seen to have acted positively, decisively and with a proper perception of the interests of others (i.e. the customers on whose satisfaction the reputation and continuation of the organisation depends) should win plaudits rather than the eventual and deserved brickbats for failing to take action. Indeed the affair ('company acting positively and compensating those affected = goods news') would probably hardly have been noticed (invariably bad news captures more attention than good).

Case study: Owning up works

In *Talking Straight* (Sidgwick & Jackson, 1988) Lee Iacocca, the man credited with having saved the Chrysler Corporation from liquidation, recounts that the organisation was selling cars that it knew had a fault as a result of some malpractice. Eventually the fault and the fact that the organisation knew of the fault became public knowledge – research indicated that 55% of the public thought the company were 'bad boys'. Chrysler decided to run an advertising campaign admitting their mistake and making the promise that it wouldn't be repeated. From a survey carried out it was clear that the public liked the fact that they were owning up – a new survey found 67% in favour of the company, a massive about-turn of public attitude.

Ripples

Unfortunately in the aftermath of a disaster there can be a large number of interested parties who need to be informed as fully as possible. Failure to inform can only generate rumour, suppositions and conjecture which once formulated can be exceedingly difficult to correct.

Example

A single-site factory has a major fire which will disrupt output for several weeks. Those needing to know the information could include

1. *Employees*

Since it may be dangerous (and pointless) for employees to attend work they should be telephoned immediately the news is known. Thereafter there will need to be CONSULTATION with them or their representatives; they will also need to be told of arrangements regarding resumption of work, short-time working, future employment/payment prospects, etc.

   Note: there are various employment law implications in this scenario which have been ignored here. Advice should be taken in such instances.

2. *Suppliers*

A manager trying to cope (for example) with the aftermath of a fire would certainly not want to deal with a delivery of raw material, with no store in which to house it. Suppliers due to deliver already ordered goods should be advised by fax, e-mail or telephone of the need to delay deliveries until further notification.

   Note: Advice might need to be taken regarding the contractual implications of delaying, and possibly cancelling, contracts.

3. *Customers*

Whilst already generated stocks might cover a hiatus in production for some time, sooner or later, there is likely to be a break in supplies. The implications of this being known (and possibly generating increased short-term demand) need to be assessed and a decision made concerning notification and the means.

4. *Sales staff*

In some respects sales staff will be covered under the information provided for employees, but since their purpose is to generate orders for goods which, whilst the factory is not operative, cannot be fulfilled, they need guidance as to their purpose in the immediate future. Again this may need to be generated using the swiftest possible means.

5. *Shareholders*

The owners of the business need to be informed of the state of their investment, although there may be little they can actually do about it. This is particularly relevant should reports of the incident be featured in local and/or national media. A printed circular using the post and/or advertisements in the press might be appropriate means for this audience.

6. *Media*

If the organisation has a high profile, or the fire was particularly spectacular, or had implications for environmental concerns, or prompted consideration of other hazards, the interest of the media will be generated. The communication means will almost certainly need to be verbal since deadlines may mitigate against delay to issue considered written statements – although these might be used for updating progress towards a resumption of normal business or for the announcement that normal business has been resumed.

Ongoing commitment

Outlined above are the communication challenges in the immediate aftermath of a disaster. However, in the event of a fire causing considerable structural damage it is possible that it could be several weeks or even months before full production is resumed. During that time the information flow will need to be maintained so that all those identified as requiring to be kept aware of what progress is being made are so informed.

Facilities

In considering informing the constituent parts of the audiences it should not be overlooked that the means by which information is regularly generated – telephone, photocopier, computer link, fax, e-mail, telex, etc., could all have been destroyed in the fire. So too could the addresses and contact numbers of the employees, suppliers, customers, etc. Indeed even the contingency plan itself might not have survived the flames. Thus consideration needs to be given to having available duplicate copies of the information and substitute facilities for immediate use. It may even be worth advertising, at least internally, an alternative telephone number should the normally used number be unobtainable. Identifying these points is relatively easy – provided there is time to spend on them.

Customer care

Introduction

As we move into the twenty-first century the balance of the terms of trade seems to be moving in favour of the consumer. An increasing number of customers are aware that their views and protests can be voiced to an organisation – and will take the opportunity, offered or not and wanted or not, of making such views known. This is particularly the case when the organisation does not seem to have provided products, services or action to the standard advertised to or expected by those customers. Organisations which value their reputation, need to try to ensure that they 'keep the customer satisfied'. Indeed, in the UK and in Europe in view of the shrinking of demand as a result of the worldwide recession of the early 1990s, simply trying to retain customers at all is a factor of economic survival. The loyalty of such customers will only be retained if they are satisfied – in many instances there is usually another supplier (and sometimes more than one) well able to grab the business if customers are dissatisfied with an organisation's performance. Unfortunately the organisation may only be aware of the reaction of a tiny proportion of its customers. The White House office of consumer affairs found in research for its Technical Assistance and Research Programme in the mid 1990s that businesses do not hear from 96% of their dissatisfied customers – and for every complaint that is received there are a further 26 silent customers of whom six have serious problems. Presumably most of this silent majority votes with its feet and/or purse in a different direction.

Reputation

Handled well, customer complaints can enhance the reputation of the organisation – handled badly, the reputation of the organisation can be severely damaged. Tony Palmer, chief executive of construction giant Taylor Woodrow, was quoted in late 1995 as saying that a good corporate image can make customers between 1% and 5% more willing to buy – often enough to tip the balance in a company's favour. Taylor Woodrow trained its 8500 staff to enhance the company's image by doing and saying the right thing. 'In interfacing with customers, we need all our staff to understand

151

public relations', Mr Palmer said. For 'understanding public relations' we could substitute 'knowing how to foster positive customer communication in all instances' and it might be beneficial to link the activities of the Customer Care and PUBLIC RELATIONS departments. Experience suggests that normally the two are remote, despite the former being probably the most important part of the latter. A dissatisfied customer is likely to tell a great number of others of the poor service or unsatisfactory treatment s/he has received – Syd Pennington, Managing Director of Virgin Atlantic, suggests that a dissatisfied customer will tell around 17 others of his bad treatment. Those who know their way around may find other outlets – consumer protection programmes on both radio and television, national press feature articles, and so on – which could increase this number dramatically. Poisoning customer demand in this way (and very often the temptation to exaggerate may not be resisted) could cost the organisation dearly – it is five times cheaper to retain an existing customer than it is to source a new one. Very often what virtually amounts to an invitation to a dissatisfied customer to 'poison the waters' is a result of the department being known as the essentially negative 'customer complaints' rather the more positive 'customer care' and treating a complaint in a cavalier and dismissive way.

Training

To ensure that customer communication is always positive, and follows management's commitment to this ideal, all employees who interface with customers need to be trained to provide a positive approach – to see the complaint through the eyes of the customer who can chose to buy or not, rather than the organisation which must sell. It might assist in commencing such training if the fact that an organisation can only survive if it satisfies and keeps satisfying its customers is the initial contention. Obviously, if enough customers are dissatisfied, there can be no employment, but despite this truism adverse reactions to customer queries is widespread in the UK – a phenomenon somewhat at variance to general experience on the Continent and in the USA. This is not to imply that every customer is always right – sometimes complaints are unjustified and unreasonable, and need to be resisted. Very often, however, observations are denied in a totally unreasonable way and the potential effect on the reputation of the business and the retention of other customers is totally overlooked. Regardless of the correctness or otherwise of the complaint, the person dealing with it needs to use tact and diplomacy and, as has been stated repeatedly in this book, to have all the facts immediately to hand.

DARN

In *Dealing with demanding customers* (Pitman, 1994) I coined the mnemonic DARN. The process of darning in needlework is to repair and make as new, and this is the underlying message of the mnemonic in the context of handling customer queries and complaints. Where customers have problems, a break has occurred in the fabric of supplier and purchaser. DARN stands for Discovery, Apology, Rectification and Novation – four stages of the process by which damaged sales 'fabric' can be repaired.

Checklist: DARN

1. By actively listening, avoiding defensive justification and asking open questions the person fielding the complaint should record the facts so that the organisation can **D** for **D**iscover and identify the problem experienced by the customer. Not only should openness, a willingness to listen and checking all the facts be undertaken, but the customer needs to see that their complaint is being taken seriously.This process can be extended to ask the customer, having gained such details, what is their desired result – what is it that they want? In this way the conversation can be converted from a 'negative complaint' to a positive 'what can we do about this' discussion.
2. If the organisation is at fault (and even if it is not or the responsibility of fault is unclear) this should generate an early **A** for **A**pology. Apologising can draw the sting from most such complaints. Faced with intransigence or negative defence of a position, it is all too easy for disappointed customers to lose their temper and become more demanding. But when the other party is apologising most people warm to them and lose their anger – rather than their temper. It can be difficult to maintain anger or annoyance when the other party seems genuinely sorry and is, apparently, trying to rectify the matter.
3. **R** for **R**ectification. Since the supplier is at fault (and even if it is not, as it may be counter-productive to dispute if the value of possible recompense is small) it should seek to make amends. Here, using the telephone to 'do a deal' with the complainant can be very useful since any offer need not be committed to paper and thus no evidence will exist for use as a precedent. This echoes the point made under D for Discover. Finding out what it is the customer wants turns the conversation into a positive mode and should disarm the most vehement complainant.
4. Finally the darning process ends with **N** for **N**ovation, which is concerned with any changes that the organisation may need to make to

the product, process, system, administration or promotional material which has been shown to be faulty. It may be that an analysis of complaints can aid the development of whatever it is that is at fault – which, of course, is part of the theory behind the use of CARELINES.

Management knowledge

Customer contacts should not be treated as a negative development – as destructive complaints from which the organisation needs protecting or defending. They can provide a valuable insight as to how the organisation and its products and employees are perceived by its customers, and details of all complaints should be regularly reviewed by senior management. If data on such problems are not reviewed and acted upon, there is little likelihood that common problems will be rectified and the incidence of complainants will almost certainly increase, at the expense of the organisation's reputation.

Charles Weiser, head of customer relations at British Airways, endorses this point. He suggested a four-point plan to convert complaining customers into repeating customers which can be summarised as follows:

1. Apologise and 'own' the problem. Complainers do not care whose fault it was – what they want is action and rectification.
2. Do something – and do it quickly. Initial satisfaction that something is being done

   - dips if customers feel they have to wait more than five days, and
   - is destroyed if they have to ring again.

3. Assure customers that the problem is being sorted. Those who are asked to deal with complaints must be fully aware of all that is going on – and particularly of changes in the products and services.
4. Phone them back – most customers appreciate personal service and a phone call can be more personal (and immediate) than a letter.

Checklist: Dealing with complaints

1. Ensure all complaints/comments/observations are recorded in a register with date (alternatively tape-record the calls).
2. Ensure some action is taken within, say, 48 hours, even if this is only an acknowledgment.
3. Research and uncover the facts, customer, order, payment record.
4. Listen carefully to the complaint, noting all relevant information.
5. Check any facts put forward or disputed by the customer.

6. Try to identify what the customer wants or needs as their desired aim. Consider whether it is possible to offer what is required.

7. Be courteous, tactful and pleasant at all times. Never raise your voice, allow irritation or anger to show, or be in any way patronising, insulting or sarcastic.

8. Don't dispute the customer's opinions – you may not agree with them but that does not automatically mean they are wrong and you are right. Arguing the point will merely worsen the situation.

9. Only if the complaint is straightforward, venture to attempt a solution and even then only after consideration of both the apparent and underlying implications.

10. If it is not possible to provide the customer's ideal solution, consider whether some compromise might be acceptable, and, if so, try to introduce the idea into the conversation.

11. In non-straightforward cases, thank the customer for bringing the matter to the organisation's attention, apologise for any inconvenience and state that the matter will be investigated rigorously and they will receive a report by [set date].

12. Ensure that the time limit by which the customer will receive an answer or further contact is observed.

13. Investigate the complaint and consider the validity of the customer's case objectively. Derive a possible response with a fall-back position if the customer refuses to accept the first suggestion.

14. Consider any precedent that might be created from a settlement and weigh against any potential backlash from publicity. Although it is often said that there is no such thing as bad publicity, this cannot be true where poor or faulty products or services can be exposed, or the safety of the consumer risked.

15. Try to conclude the dispute harmoniously, with the aim of enhancing the reputation of the organisation.

Phoning back

Phoning the customer back can be very valuable. The fact that

- someone has taken the trouble to make the call,
- a real person is speaking who at least appears to be really involved with the problem, and
- individual attention is being given to the matter rather than the matter being dealt with by a standard-response letter with an indecipherable signature can be very valuable. Using the phone allows input from the customer whilst conversely using a standard letter conveys the hidden

message – 'here is our response, we've heard it all before, go away (satisfied or not)' – which is hardly the best approach to a representative of those on whose custom the success of the organisation may depend.

Commitment

Rather than setting up a system for dealing with customer complaints it may be preferable to adopt a complaint conversion programme.

Example: Customer complaints conversion (CCC) policy

Our operation is geared to satisfying our customers since it is only through satisfying our customers and more of them that we can pay for everything on which we spend company money, including of course our own wages.

It is cheaper to retain an existing customer than it is to source a new customer.

It is our policy to encourage contact with customers so that

1. The company obtains feedback from the marketplace – since unless we know precisely how the marketplace views our products/services we cannot develop and improve them.

2. Problems and queries related to our products and services are brought to the company's attention for positive rectification.

3. Positive customer satisfaction is generated with both our products and our after-sales service.

4. CCC has several functions:

- to create a rapport with the customer and marketplace
- to discover the true nature of problems
- to discuss/decide any contribution to any loss suffered
- to attempt to retain the customer for repeat sales
- to preserve the company's reputation, and
- to consider whether it is necessary to implement any design changes as a result of the information generated.

Departmental newsletters

Introduction

The JOURNALS AND NEWSLETTERS section provides guidance on how to generate the compilation of such documents on an ongoing and organisation-wide basis, as well as how to promote them. However, there seems little doubt that for specific purposes (e.g. during a period of substantial and rapid change, during major building work or a relocation, and so on) where information of record needs to be disseminated with little necessity for feedback, issuing brief updates of progress can be an effective means of ensuring that those immediately affected are kept up to date. Alternatively, and particularly where employees are working far from the main organisations (e.g. field staff, sales representatives, etc.), it can be helpful to generate such newsletters as part of the overall communication procedure. Finally newsletters that relate solely to particular areas or divisions within the business can be a powerful communicative channel.

Contribution

Newsletters, being written and consisting largely of 'non-feedback' material tend to be well down most employees' order of preferred means of 'communication'. This, however, can be compensated, at least in part, by encouraging employees to write for the item themselves. Where both corporate and local newsletters exist many employees' preference is for the local version, since, not surprisingly, they are able to identify with it to a far greater extent than with the corporate version. Provided the amount of business news is restricted to not much more than 25–30%, that the style is informal, that illustrations and colour (even if only a single additional colour) are used and that the employees are encouraged to write part of it themselves (and thus are seen to 'own' it and identify with it) then the document can play a valuable role in creating rapport and understanding. If employees are both readers and writers then what is essentially a one-way information provider can be converted to a two-way communication tool.

Procedure

To explain the philosophy, as well as promoting the concept that a departmental issue is envisaged and that contributions are welcomed, the generation and promulgation of a policy/procedure such as is shown in the following checklist may be helpful.

Checklist: Local newsletter policy/procedure

1. Whilst the [organisation] sponsors the production of [name] as its in-house journal and encourages employees to contribute articles for inclusion, it is recognised that at times there is a need for employees in individual working groups to have available a regular flow of written information specifically applicable to that work group and/or location.

2. Accordingly heads of divisions are encouraged to authorise the production of information newsletter(s) and/or local newsletter(s) to achieve this.

3. Such newsletters should be produced internally using in-house word-processing and desktop publishing materials and software. All costs are to be borne by the department/division for which the item is intended.

4. Sufficient copies should be generated to provide one for every employee within the work group for which they are presented, plus copies for all concerned with BRIEFING GROUPS covering those employees, and copies for the editor of the [organisation]-wide journal.

   Note: Copies should be provided for the editor of the journal as a data source in case an article of interest on an organisation-wide basis can be generated by the subject matter.

5. Managers using the system should be aware that nothing printed should be expected to remain confidential within [the organisation]. In generating written material which may be sensitive or otherwise contain information regarded as confidential they should therefore expect it to find its way to an outside source and be appropriately circumspect regarding any such material.

6. A master copy of all items generated should be kept by the manager concerned for [specify period] after the conclusion of the project being reviewed.

7. Employees should be invited to contribute to regularly produced newsletter(s) on the same basis as they are for the corporate newsletter.

8. The language used should be kept to ordinary everyday English, avoiding (or explaining) all JARGON. A light-hearted (but not flippant) style should be used and ideally the amount of work-based data should

be restricted to around one-quarter (although this rule should be relaxed where the subject matter is essentially an update of information related to a particular project).

9. All employees within the target group should be encouraged to write for their newsletter with appropriate sources always being acknowledged. The guidance provided for writers for the organisation's JOURNAL should be used.

10. Those responsible for editing the newsletter should exercise judgement concerning the inclusion of items. If it is decided not to use an item, the person submitting it should be informed of the reason.

Disciplinary interviews

Introduction

Although many will regard a disciplinary interview as an essentially private matter between manager and employee, in some cases it is possible for there ultimately to be a public dimension. The record and outcome of an interview handled badly (that is, not in accordance with an employer's procedure and/or legal requirements) could one day be inspected by an Industrial Tribunal and even by the national media as their interest in tribunal cases continues to grow. There is thus a potential for considerable damage being caused to the reputation of the employing organisation if such events are poorly handled. Indeed, should an organisation gain a reputation for being a poor employer not only could morale suffer (which itself could lead to further disciplinary problems, increased absenteeism and petty pilfering, etc.) and increased labour turnover, but also difficulty could well be experienced in attracting new applicants.

Purpose

It can be argued that there are two main reasons for disciplinary interviews being necessary: (1) to state that an employee is not performing or behaving in the desired fashion and to demonstrate how this can be rectified; and (2) to prepare a case that could ultimately lead to dismissal. Unfortunately some employers tend to regard such interviews as solely of the latter variety. In 1996 Dr Derek Rollinson canvassed the opinions of over 100 employees who had been subject to their employers' disciplinary processes. Many felt that their cases had been dealt with in an unfair way. Only 24% stated that they now observed the rules they had been disciplined for breaking, whilst a further 24% stated that they obeyed the rules grudgingly. The employees who had changed their habits to avoid breaching the rules stated that their managers had taken a persuasive line 'sometimes spending more than an hour getting the employee to understand that a rule had been breached'.

In most other cases the employees felt the managers had assumed guilt and were simply going through the motions. The hidden messages from these approaches are obvious – and can be easily understood by employees other than those disciplined.

Procedure

All such interviews should be conducted exactly in accordance with the procedure laid down by the employer. Thus the procedure itself needs to be clear and concise and to be made available to all. In addition those who need to apply it in practice need to be coached so that their actions, each in exact accordance with it, occur automatically as routine.

WARNING: Ideally a disciplinary procedure (and especially any appeal procedure) should be kept as short as (and with as few options as) possible. The more complex a procedure is, the more likely it is that at some stage there may be an unintended deviation from it by either party. Should the employer deviate from the procedure they may be unable to defend their actions successfully in a tribunal.

Although it is not a legal requirement, an employee should always be offered the opportunity of being accompanied by a representative to act as their witness. There is no need for the witness to say anything, although it may be helpful if they make notes of what transpires.

Record

Notes (ideally a verbatim record) should be kept of the proceedings and it is helpful if the employee is given a copy and requested within a specified time (e.g. two working days) to confirm that the notes are a true record of what transpired. Should the employee challenge the record it should be corrected unless the chairman of the proceedings feels the challenge /alteration is unwarranted.

> Note: The advantage of making a verbatim record of such interviews is that composing a record from notes may 'place into the mouth of the employee' words and sentiments which are not his/hers but rather interpretation (even a translation) of what s/he said. Should the employee later challenge the record, it may be difficult for the employer to convince third parties that the record was entirely accurate.

Case study: Unbelievable

In a tribunal case concerning a dismissal following a scuffle between two employees – both over six feet tall and one of whom weighed around 18 stone – the record of a disciplinary interview lasting two hours placed before the tribunal was just two pages long. It contained so-called quotes from the applicant (who had been dismissed despite there having been extreme provocation) including

'he (the 18 stone employee) swore and squared up to me and I subtly pushed him away'

'he had previously put his hands in my pockets to which I had to retaliate as I am sensitive' and

'I think the problem was that we emanated from different cultures.'

The applicant was an immigrant and English was not his native tongue. He was a shy man who had difficulty reading and expressing himself. The tribunal found it difficult to imagine him using words such as 'subtly' (particularly in the context of being squared up to by someone of the other's size), 'sensitive' and 'emanated'. In turn this raised severe doubts about the accuracy of the record.

With the availability of cheap tape-recording facilities it may be advisable to tape-record interviews concerned with more serious allegations. If this alternative is used then it would be advisable to make two machines available so that a copy is available for the employee immediately at the conclusion of the proceedings (as is the case following police interviews). A typed transcript of every word can then be prepared and since two copies exist it will be difficult for this record to be challenged. In addition not only should the words be recorded but so also can the tone and inflexions which can alter the words themselves.

Decision

Once all witnesses have been heard and each side has been able to question them, and an opportunity has been given to each side to make final submissions (which in the employee's case might include a plea for leniency should his/her previous record have been good), a decision will need to be made. It may be helpful to adjourn whilst the chairman considers the evidence and a suitable penalty. This has the advantage of demonstrating (or at least implying) that justice is being done. The decision should be recorded in writing, particularly if any penalty is involved, since this should minimise the possibility of dispute about the result.

Appeal

As mentioned above, rules concerning appeals should be kept as brief and clear as possible and very few restrictions should be applied. Indeed there is an argument for providing internal advice regarding lodging an appeal to ensure fairness. Rejecting an application for appeal requires explanation and carries an automatic inference of unfairness. Allowing an appeal to be heard, even one of dubious merit, conveys the message that here is an employer determined to be fair. These hidden messages can contain very powerful inferences for those watching the transaction.

The hidden watchers

Although a disciplinary interview may be handled with discretion and a degree of confidentiality, inevitably in most instances details of the 'offence' and the decision will be rumoured, and inevitably, since such decisions provide proof of the attitude of the employer, will be the subject of considerable interest. For this reason proceedings and decisions need to be

- entirely in accordance with the procedure
- fair and reasoned and sustainable in terms of precedent
- in keeping with the rules and regulations of the employer.

In addition the decisions – warnings, suspension, dismissal, etc., – need to be both fair and to be seen to be fair.

Guidance

It may be helpful to keep a central record of interviews so that those managers needing to conduct such hearings can read first-hand accounts of previous instances and obtain an insight into the way the organisation wishes interviews to be conducted. Exercising control over and applying sanctions to employees is a right of every employer – but this right entails considerable responsibilities to ensure fairness and consistency. Getting it wrong can send a variety of messages to interested parties.

Employee reports

Introduction

Research indicates that in companies where employees understand the financial results, productivity and motivation is higher than elsewhere, particularly where disclosure of such information has been required because share or share-option schemes have been introduced. Generating meaningful information to the non-financially aware may pose a problem since few ANNUAL REPORTS, the normal source of such figures, are presented in a form capable of being understood other than by accountants and those similarly trained. A survey conducted by MORI disclosed that only 20% of shareholders claimed to have read most or all of their companies' Annual Reports. Another survey found that, when questioned, less than a third of the 75% of shareholders who claimed to have read the report displayed a 'reasonable grasp of the contents'. If the aim of the company is to report to its employees it is logical that such a report should be designed and presented with the interests and requirements of that audience in mind.

Background

Companies have been producing employee reports, whether known by such a title or not, for over 100 years. However, the movement gathered momentum in the 1970s and 1980s when around 500 PLCs as well as an equal number of private limited companies were producing them each year. Since then the numbers have fallen somewhat, although annual competitions still attract around 100 entries and there are many companies who do not enter. Once such a report has been introduced as part of the communication data it can be difficult to dispense with it since

- such documents can attract considerable interest from the target audience, and
- their production generates a demand which needs satisfying.

Legal obligations

Under the Employment Act 1982 there is an obligation on every company employing more than 250 employees to include in its Directors' Report a statement describing the action it has taken during the financial period under review to introduce, maintain or develop arrangements aimed at

- providing employees systematically with information on matters of concern to them as employees
- consulting employees on a regular basis so that their views can be taken into account in making decisions which are likely to affect their interest
- encouraging the involvement of employees in the company's performance through an employee share scheme or by some other means and
- achieving a common awareness on the part of all employees of the financial and economic factors affecting the performance of the company.

Employee reports are not subject to Companies Act legislation or to Statutory Standards of Accounting Practice, although, under the Companies Act 1985, there is a requirement to state in the report that the figures are an extract from the full report which has been lodged with the Registrar of Companies.

Aim of the report

Basically to comply with the foregoing one could define the aim of such a report as being 'the means by which the financial results, statistics and commentary can be presented in such a way that they can be understood by everyone'. 'Everyone' in this context refers particularly to the layman and non-accountant. Obviously this poses a considerable challenge to the editor or author since those who are experienced in clarity of communication presentation may not be proficient in accountancy, whilst those proficient in accountancy may not be able to produce the 'user-friendly overview' that is needed or able to demonstrate the significance of the figures to a layman.

Content

The following checklist of contents should be used as a guide – from which a majority of the items should be selected for inclusion. The need is to produce a report which explains the salient features of the results.

Checklist: Content of simplified report

1.   Statements of the aims of the business and of the report
2.   Statement by the chairman in ordinary English avoiding JARGON
3.   Highlights of the year
4.   Balance sheet (with an explanation of the terms used)
5.   Simplified profit and loss account or Added Value statement
6.   Statement of sales and profit, particularly expressed per employee, and possibly showing the effect of inflation – on a localised or divisional basis
7.   General information regarding products or services, employees, share schemes, environmental and community matters, etc.
8.   ORGANISATION CHART(S)
9.   Comment on future plans or developments
10. GRAPHICS and illustrations supporting and complementing the above items.

> Note: *Since most readers 'minds' eyes' can capture trends and proportions far more easily if expressed in graphic form than in a line or list of figures/text, the use of clear uncomplicated graphics should help achieve better reader comprehension. To add detail, the definition set out in the paragraph under the heading 'Aim of the report' (p. 166) could be expanded as follows:*

1.   *'. . . financial results . . . '*
     The financial results of a company can be reported in a number of ways

     • as actuals
     • by comparison with previous results and
     • by comparison with a previous projection.

     Obviously the figures must be the same as those in the annual report, and, in order to demonstrate progress (or lack of it), a comparison with at least the previous year's figures may be helpful. Only rarely will an annual report refer to a detailed projection given previously, and it may be better to avoid including such figures, though should the results be at variance to any previously indicated, the variation should be addressed and explained.

     It is customary in an annual report for five (or even ten) years results to be shown in a single chart. Whilst these may be useful as a broad indication of progress (although since rarely is any adjustment made for inflation such charts may be less meaningful than should be the case) these may be better not used in an employee report. Employees tend to be more interested in 'tomorrow' rather than 'yesterday'.

2.   *'. . . statistics . . .'*
     Statistics abound in an annual report but relatively few of these may be of real interest other than

167

- those directly related to his/her work/department/shop/depot, etc.
- those showing how they fit into the whole
- those indicating the future.

In each case it will help if the figures used are of a size to which people can relate. Research indicates that many employees cannot fully relate to a figure much in excess of the value of the average house (i.e. probably most employees' largest item of expenditure) – although the success of the National Lottery may have changed this perception. If this is so then the use of illustrations reducing figures (often running into millions) to £1, £10 or £100 units, and utilising proportions of the base figure to represent items of income, expenditure, etc., may be most effective.

3. *'. . . commentary . . .'*

An explanation of, and the significance of, 'what happened' in the last year – and 'what is anticipated might happen in the coming year' – will normally be the items which gain most attention. Although the figures are the obvious evidence of achievement, only the commentary can provide a guide as to what the figures 'mean'. A statement from the chairman or chief executive, provided it is specially written for this report and is not simply a rehash (or worse, a reprint) of the annual report statement, can be especially valuable in view of the extra credence that will be given a statement emanating from this source.

Care must be taken in drafting such a statement which must be user-friendly. It should be factual and 'honest' – in the sense that the statement must not patronise the audience, and neither should it contain hype or be in any way a vehicle for management propaganda. If the target audience feel they are being patronised, or subjected to hype or propaganda not only will the report lose its credibility and fail to be read (and thus fail in its prime purpose) but also any rapport that existed between employees and management will almost certainly disappear. There is very little point in trying to hype employees – they know the organisation too well.

4. *'. . . understood by everyone . . .'*

Whilst some annual reports are commendable for their use of ordinary English, many use jargon. Although jargon can be a useful form of verbal or written shorthand and may be acceptable when everyone involved is aware of the meaning of the words, it should either be avoided, or (if this is impossible), explained in the text.

Clarity

Attempting to entice and to retain the attention of a target audience, many of whose members will not be used to studying financial data, is a

168

considerable challenge and can only be answered by ensuring the utmost clarity of the concept and presentation. In the author's book *Financial Reporting to Employees* (Gee 1997) the following checklist of considerations was recommended for use in compiling such material:

Checklist: Presentation considerations for production of an employee report

1. KISS: KISS in this context stands for 'keep it short and simple'. An alternative version admonishes us to 'keep it simple, stupid'.

   Writing in this way you may be criticised by some but at least you should be capable of being understood by all. Written material does not necessarily become easier to understand if it is made longer. Indeed, research indicates that on average attention from and retention by the target audience, decreases in direct proportion to the length of the content. A message, article or report on a single sheet of paper is far more likely to gain and retain attention than an item several times its size.

2. Make the content enticing – use headlines and other 'text signposts' to avoid the reader's eye being repelled by masses of uninviting text, and to direct their attention to those items that interest them most.

3. Decide on the message, write that message and then check that what you have written conveys your original intended message. If it does, use it, if not remember the Robert E. Lee rule. General Lee always chose as his batman a man who was not particularly bright. Then when he wrote an order he would show it to his batman and ask the batman to tell him what it meant. Only if the batman told him what he had intended the order to mean did Lee publish the order – if not he rewrote it. (Sometimes of course one has insufficient time for such a process – which may explain why Lee lost the war!)

4. Keep the target audience and their requirements in mind. If they are college professors or lawyers they should be able to handle complex written material and indeed may prefer their data presented in this way. It is unlikely that the same is true of the average employee. The content must be user-friendly and user-aimed.

5. Use short sentences. Complex sentences tend to confuse the average reader. If the reader has to re-read the sentence to try and understand the meaning
   - firstly it means that the writer has failed, and
   - secondly it may irritate the reader so much that his/her attention is lost – not only to that sentence but also to the rest of the item. Short sentences are more effective when trying to make important points.

6. Don't become trapped into overusing the same words – particularly verbs. Constantly using the same verbs makes the copy boring.

7. Don't link dissimilar ideas – apart from the fact this can make sentences overlong, the dissimilarity of the content can confuse. Whilst useful as a general rule this is essential in terms of financial reporting – particularly when using graphics.

8. Avoid using nouns as verbs. Verbs are the 'doing' words and should be used in that context. 'After lunch we will car the group to Factory X' may be shorter than 'After lunch the group will be taken by car to Factory X' but the latter is unlikely to be misunderstood, whilst the former makes the reader wonder if the typist meant to insert 'carry' which then makes the wording so fascinating that the required attention to the message may be lost!

9. Don't use JARGON (unless the only readers are those familiar with its use and you can be confident everyone understands what it means) or prefabricated phrases.

10. Avoid prefabricated phrases, buzz words or the definitions beloved of the 'politically correct' movement. Many of these tend to be imprecise and may cause irritation. An irritated reader will quickly cease to be a reader.

11. Avoid using 'flannel' or 'hype'. 'Flannel' means using phrases and language which say little but try to cover up the reality whereas 'hype' is short for hyperbole which means 'a phrase which is exaggerated but is not meant to be taken seriously'.

12. Don't try to rewrite history. In writing for external publication most authors will wish to show the organisation in a good light – this is a situation which most employees can readily appreciate. However, in writing communication material for internal consumption, such revised versions are (like hype) unacceptable. Truth, honesty and consistency are needed.

Summary financial statements

Since 1990 PLCs have been able to send those shareholders who so elect, a summary financial statement (SFS). The concept of such a document is that it should provide an overview of the results without the detail that is normally included in an annual report. Inevitably since both an SFS and an employee report seek to provide user-friendly versions of the financial results document there is similarity in their approach. However, the number of companies who produce an SFS is relatively small and since some of them run to more than 40 pages it seems that their whole rationale has been subsumed in the detail they were meant to avoid!

External actions

Introduction

The skills and examples of approach contained here are aimed at helping organisations seeking to improve internal and external communication in the widest sense of the word. In most cases what is required is positive action in order to achieve the aim of the particular item. However, messages are generated and conveyed by every action and attitude, and the effect of this, especially with regard to giving out potentially negative messages, needs to be taken into account. Whilst an organisation may struggle to find what it believes to be the ideal wording to incorporate in a PRESS RELEASE seeking to 'tell the world' about something which reflects well on it, it is often overlooked that its actions in other arenas may show a far more accurate insight to its real, 'unhyped', attitudes. Whilst customers and suppliers will watch for signals to indicate the current approach of the organisation, no one may watch the signals more closely than its own employees. Equally no one can do more to ensure the success or otherwise of an organisation than its employees.

Taking action

The ramifications of employment law are such that many employers need to appear in an Industrial Tribunal to defend their actions. Such is the complexity of the law that even organisations which are correctly regarded as 'models of good employment principles and practice' have needed to defend tribunal actions, and several have lost such cases. The problem for the employer is that the very fact of appearing may be seen as adverse by many employees, whilst the circumstances of the case, since the vast majority of such cases are open to the public and many are reported in the local and national media, are available for all to review and consider.

Case study: Physician heal thyself

A semi-voluntary organisation which had as its function and aim the attempt to combat racial discrimination, was found by a tribunal to have sexually discriminated against one of its employees. The publicity given the case caused the major backers of the organisation to withdraw, which in turn led to the collapse of the organisation itself.

In that instance the fact that an organisation which had set itself up with the aim of combating discrimination had actually broken the law, the effect of which it was set up to promote, might generate little sympathy from onlookers for the outcome. However, it would certainly have sent an adverse message to potential female employees. On a more basic level, however, organisations may send adverse signals to their employees.

Case study: Hypocritical?

a) A leading company known for its positive and progressive employment practices was found to have unfairly dismissed an employee who was injured (and eventually unable to resume her normal job) whilst trying to protect her employer's goods from a thief.

b) A company refused to pay Statutory Sick Pay to an employee who injured her back whilst working for them. Their point was that she was employed on a daily contract and thus did not accrue the three months' service necessary to enable her to claim SSP. The Court of Appeal held her eight months' service on single-day contracts was 'continuous' and thus she was entitled to be paid.

c) An employer refused to allow a woman the holiday to which she was entitled because it had accrued during the time she was on maternity leave. The legislation states that a woman is entitled to all 'non-monetary' benefits at such a time. Her claim was upheld.

The exact circumstances of these cases do not concern us here. Indeed such circumstances will not concern most of those who will read or hear about the decisions, as they will tend to judge on the effect rather than the reasons, and are very unlikely to appreciate their organisation's concern for the creation of precedents, etc. In each case the employer could be regarded by many as 'doing the wrong thing' which sends messages to all listeners. It would be hardly surprising if the reaction to such cases was negative, and as a result morale and commitment to the organisations were impaired. Were these the kind of messages the organisations wished to send, not just to their employees but also to all others doing business with them?

Make the decision

It may of course be that there were precedents which needed to be protected, or principles to be maintained which led to the above cases being fought. If this was the case, and the decision was taken at the top of the organisation, then hopefully the effect of losing was taken into account and the cases were thought to be worth the cost of resisting.

Case study: Was it worth it?

When a manager left his high-profile company he objected to the fact that his accrued holiday pay entitlement was calculated by dividing his annual salary by 365 to obtain a day's rate. Since he only worked around 260 days each year he felt that should be the divisor – as it is for many organisations. The company resisted the claim up to the Employment Appeal Tribunal. Even though they won the argument the costs involved must have been considerable – the amount at stake in terms of the holiday pay was £130.

The decision to resist what seems a reasonable claim as regards the calculation of holiday pay (or to dismiss a long-serving employee injured trying to protect the property of the business, or not to pay sickness benefit to a person injured at work, or not to abide by legislation requiring the preservation of benefits) could create adverse comment – not just from employees, but also from others (customers, suppliers, shareholders, etc.) becoming aware of the actions since the media are increasingly giving prominence to the decisions of tribunals.

Of course it is not only in the field of employee relations that such 'messages' can be publicised. An organisation which gains a reputation for not paying its accounts promptly, or for always dealing harshly with those with whom it does business (whether buying or selling), or which refuses to support local charitable activities can swiftly build a reputation at variance to, but possibly more accurate than, that which it may strive to give through its PUBLIC RELATIONS programme.

The contents of the following checklist are pertinent.

Checklist: External action authority

All decisions which may result in legal action or generate publicity and public attention should only be taken

(a) at a senior level in the organisation [by name/position], and

(b) after a full assessment has been made of the financial effect of the decision, the precedent involved and the effect of the result of the action on both internal and external audiences.

Handbooks

Introduction

Understanding the meaning of information presented in a written form is more difficult than when such information is presented in an individual face-to-face encounter, or even in a presentation at which those attending have an opportunity to input their own questions and views. However, realistically, in many instances there is no real alternative to using the written word. If it is important that the target audience read and understand the content in order to comply with the requirements of or understand the terms of the organisation, or understand the operation of products, etc., a user-friendly handbook is essential. Such a handbook will usually contain the guidance as to the manner in which employees are expected to behave, procedures, prohibitions, etc. Even though there may be verbal presentations on the subject, each employee should have his/her own copy of the handbook and there needs to be a procedure which checks that employees not only have a copy but have read and understood the requirements placed upon them.

Providing the data

As well as an understanding of 'the way we do things round here' there is a vast amount of data that needs to be imparted to employees, particularly newcomers. This problem is compounded by the fact that people will need different information at different times, although there may be a fair amount of common ground. Few people, particularly when new to an organisation, can absorb too much of even the most essential information at one time and thus need material to which they can refer as and when necessary.

Presentation

Employee handbooks can be typed (and either bound or left in a loose-leaf format) or printed (and again either bound or loose-leaf). They could also be made available in electronic format where most or all employees operate display screens. If an electronic format is provided then so too should a hard copy be available, not only for those who do not have immediate access to a screen, but also since research indicates that few people like reading from a screen.

Whilst a bound book may be easier to carry around and refer to, it can become outdated very quickly. Conversely a loose-leaf format may tend to be bulkier but will allow for updating without replacing the whole. Using an electronic mail format should enable the item to be updated easily, but unless an item(s) is printed off when required, it may be difficult to achieve the portability and/or accessibility of the subject and other pages which are available in the printed format.

Disparate handbooks

In a group organisation with several parts or divisions it may be that each has different (or additional) rules and requirements – indeed this may be so even for different grades within a single unit. To avoid a multiplicity of handbooks there could be a standard version containing rules, etc., common to all. Supplements (possibly on coloured paper) can then be used to display additional data as applicable to each individual part. If the standard handbook is designed with a pocket or retaining flap this supplementary, division-specific information can be inserted there. If a loose-leaf format is used this is unlikely to be too much of a problem, although the need to ensure the correct rules appear in the right version is paramount.

Content

The suggested outline contents for an employee handbook are as follows, (although it must be stressed that the actual content is something for individual employers to determine):

- index (as most documents will be of at least a dozen pages some alphabetical guide may be helpful. An index provides the instant guide even if the contents are themselves arranged alphabetically.
- introduction (or statement of what is trying to be achieved)
- message from employer
- individual data
- ORGANISATION CHART
- general information about employer, products, etc.
- rules and regulations
- policies where it is essential (or legally required) that these are made available to all employees (for example the disciplinary policy)

An outline content of what might be included in a handbook is shown in the following checklist.

Checklist: Commonly included handbook terms

1. *Absence* (due to illness) – initial notification, keeping employer informed, documentation required, length, etc.
2. *Access to personnel file* – rights to view computerised and (from 1998) manual data kept by the employer
3. *Address* – marriage, next of kin, other changes of personal information; need to advise such changes
4. *Advertising* – ban on using company premises for own without permission
5. *Appeals procedure* – if not covered by *grievance procedure* (see below)
6. *Canteen* – arrangements, subsidy, etc.
7. *Communication* – company commitment to
8. *Consumption of alcohol/use of non-medicinal drugs* – banning subject to disciplinary action
9. *Contract of employment* – arrangements for issue
10. *Disciplinary rules* – complete disciplinary procedure and application
11. *Disclosure of company information* – need to preserve confidentiality
12. *Dishonesty* – company attitude to
13. *Doctor* – arrangements re using company doctor and company right to ask for report from such doctor
14. *Equal opportunities* – complete procedure and recital of policy which should address bullying, unfair criticism, harassment, initiation rites, etc.
15. *Extended leave* – arrangements and controls or prohibition
16. *Fire procedure* – complete procedure
17. *First aid* – arrangements and controls
18. *Grievance procedure* – complete policy and procedure, stressing urge to use system whenever necessary
19. *Health and Safety policy* – complete policy and procedure, reference to elected representatives, etc.
20. *Holidays* – arrangements, controls
21. *Hours of work* – arrangements, possible reminder of need for punctuality
22. *Hygiene, cleanliness and tidiness* – requirements
23. *Joint consultative committee* (or Works Council) – commitment, terms of reference, arrangements for elections, etc.
24. *Leave of absence* (compassionate) – arrangements and control
25. *Lost property* – arrangements for collection and claiming, employer's limit of liability
26. *Maternity* – reference to need to consult in view of complexity, etc.

27. *Overtime* – control (usually to be specifically authorised in advance), confirmation of rates
28. O*wn property protection* – restriction of company liability
29. *Pay* – arrangements
30. *Pension scheme* – reference to detailed rules of scheme, advice *re* contact, etc., arrangements for election of member trustees
31. *People relationships* – need to relate to others
32. *Personal problems* – details of counselling services available
33. *Promotion* – policy *re* internal advancement
34. *Protective clothing* – requirements regarding wearing
35. *Punctuality – tidiness* and guidance on requirements
36. *Purchase of company products* – arrangements, possible link with precautions against theft
37. *Raffles* – banning unless specific permission granted
38. *Redundancy* – arrangements, election of representatives for consultation
39. *Repairs to machinery* – banning employees' attempts other than those specifically required to carry out such work
40. *Retirement* – arrangements
41. *Right of search* – arrangements
42. *Save it!* – need to conserve energy, raw materials, etc.
43. *Smoking* – restrictions within company premises
44. *Social activities* – arrangements and outline of timetable, contact names
45. *Systems, procedures and products* – encouragement to employees to make suggestions *re* improving
46. *Theft* – company attitude *re* prosecution
47. *Training policy* – complete guidance with link with *appraisal* if in operation.

Size

The actual size and presentation of the handbook can give an impression of the approach and ethos. Thus in a small company an A5 document might be appropriate, particularly as there are likely to be fewer policy items and rules than would be found in a larger company. A5 also has the advantage of slipping easily into pockets or handbags. Conversely it has the disadvantage of needing to use smaller type to cover the content. Larger and more complex organisations will normally wish to use A4 which is a standard size, fitting most files and filing drawers.

Layout and language

The following guidelines should be addressed.

Checklist: Handbook layout guidelines

1. Pages should be well-spaced with good use of headlines, subheadlines and visual impact – that is, leaving plenty of white paper to avoid the page looking cramped.
2. Bite-sized chunks of text – say not more than 100 words in the average paragraph – should be used so that the content is easy to digest.
3. Sentences which can be understood at first reading should always be used – this indicates a need to use sentences which are simple (i.e. having an average length of around 30 words) rather than long, complex sentences.

   Note: As an example, sentence 3 contains 36 words, whilst sentences 1, 2 and 3 together contain 87 words.

4. A decent-sized and plain-type font should be used.
5. Present lines of type containing not more than 65 characters so that the eye can retain register on the lines even in lengthy paragraphs.
6. Jargon should be avoided, or, if it is unavoidable, a glossary explaining it should be provided.
7. Ideally each item should start on a new page to give it the prominence it needs. If this is impractical there should be a distinguishable gap between each item and the next.
8. Items should be arranged alphabetically for ease of location.

Generally the language should be ordinary everyday English, although should the workforce contain representatives whose mother tongue is not English it may be necessary to produce a foreign language version. (See INTERNATIONAL CHALLENGES)

Colour

Colour is a powerful means of attracting and retaining reader attention, and, used carefully, it can add considerably to the appeal of the handbook. It may be more expensive than simply using black on white but it can help to

- provide emphasis
- break up heavy text
- draw attention to key areas, etc.

Even if four-colour printing cannot be afforded, the addition of a single colour (e.g. the dominant corporate colour) can assist in this regard.

If the cost of even one additional colour cannot be justified, coloured paper could be used to differentiate sections of the text. This could echo any colour-coding used when posting NOTICES.

Because colour-coding is so effective, strict observance is necessary to ensure only items appropriate to the colour chosen appear on that colour paper, or else confusion will result.

Issue

If a handbook is to be issued where none has previously existed, a communication exercise explaining its purpose and advantages should be undertaken. Human beings are creatures of habit, and change virtually of any type tends to be regarded with suspicion and resisted if not introduced carefully. When such changes affect the employer–employee relationship, susceptibilities need to be taken into account, suspicions need to be allayed and reassurance provided.

Revision

Nothing undermines the credibility of a document more effectively than the knowledge that it contains out-of-date information – particularly rules. Unfortunately personnel law and administration is subject to so much and so rapid alteration that changes will almost certainly be necessary on a regular basis. However, a constant flood of minor alterations will add nothing to the value of the document – and indeed could be detrimental. Accordingly, it may be helpful

(a) where a fundamental rule has changed to update it immediately, but
(b) where the data is more information-based, to batch changes, so that only two or three updates are issued each year.

It may also be wise to state in the handbook that there will be changes and commit to updates as set out in (a) and (b) plus, say, a two-yearly total revision – in this way employees will be encouraged to expect rather than suspect changes. The handbook may also be more acceptable to employees if they are invited to comment on, or make suggestions for, alterations or improvements. Even if such suggestions are not taken up, explanation of the reason for the refusal can help comprehension of the position and communication generally.

Induction

Introduction

First impressions make a considerable impact – and there is only one chance to make a first impression. The way newcomers to the organisation are treated is all-important since research indicates that a majority of failed recruitments occur within the first year of employment. Whilst inevitably some resignations result from a simple mismatch of the parties concerned, others occur because not enough has been done to introduce the new recruit to the organisation, to ensure they settle down, and to give them support whilst they learn the requirements of their job and begin to understand 'the way things are done around here'. A majority of recruits, regardless of what they may say to the contrary, do find it difficult to settle and to adapt. If this is important in terms of the individual, it may be equally important in terms of the organisation.

The process

Ideally the full induction process should be structured and spread over the entire first year of employment as is suggested in the checklist below. Whilst this level of time-investment may surprise some, the costs of recruiting, on-the-job coaching (whether structured or not), mistakes of those learning the job, and so on, are so considerable (in 1997 retailers W. H. Smith calculated that it cost them around £3000 to recruit a shop assistant) that any reduction is likely to be cost-effective.

Checklist: Structuring the introduction process

Stage 1

An **introduction** period covering the time from the conclusion of the final interview, the period of offer and acceptance, and up to and including arrival. Whilst care must be taken not to overload the appointee, if information can be given to them prior to the start date the process of assimilation can start that much earlier.

Stage 2

An **induction** period covering the time from arrival to, say, the end of the second month of employment, when a great deal of information must be absorbed so that the recruit can actually begin to work effectively.

> *Note:* *The adoption of such a period links with the legal requirement to provide the contract documentation by the end of the eighth week of employment.*

Stage 3

An **instruction** period covering the time from the beginning of the third month to the end of first year of employment. The aim during this time is to enable the new employee to become completely at ease in their environment, increasingly productive and to prepare them for their first appraisal which may generate further training needs.

Information transfer

During each of these three stages various items need to be explained and the recruit's comprehension checked. To ensure such comprehension certain items can be duplicated at subsequent stages, as shown in the following checklist. Further, the fact that there is constant interfacing should enable reinforcement of the requirements of rules to take place. Some rule infringements are simply a question of adopting bad habits – avoidance of which can render unnecessary some disciplinary encounters.

Checklist: Induction

Recruit's name	Introduction	Induction	Instruction
Offer letter/confirmation	/		
Draft contract sent	/		
Handbook/rules/information	/	/	/
		(knowledge)	(familiarity)
Reception – time	/		
– place	/		
– P45/P46	/		
– C383	/		
– SSP(1)L	/	/	
– P38(S)	/		
– Disabled person	/		
– Engagement form	/	/	
Access/clock card	/		
Toilets	/	/	

	1	2	3
Changing rooms	/	/	
Locker-key	/		
Car-park pass	/		
Telephone	/		
Discount card	/		
Confidentiality undertaking	/	/	
Sickness administration	/	/	/
Fire alarm	/	/	/
Safety matters	/	/	/
Wage advance	/		
Department introduction		/	
Local facilities (vending, toilets, etc.)		/	
Person introduction		/	
Job introduction		/	/
Timekeeping and breaks		/	
Organisational rules	/	/	/
Departmental rules	/	/	/
Discipline and procedure	/	/	/
Grievance and procedure	/	/	/
Tour local departments		/	
Payslip		/	
Organisation chart		/	/
Relationship chart	/	/	
Training		/	/
Interrelated departments introduction		/	/
Induction course			/
Tour of premises			/
Questions	/	/	/

Notes:

1. *Either the immediate supervisor or manager (or MENTOR) needs to cross tick to show that the item has been covered with the recruit. If a tick appears in more than one column, then the person responsible for each subsequent part of the process is expected to recheck knowledge.*

2. *Ideally each employee should be asked to confirm that he/she has been taken through the items on each list – possibly by signing the checklist. It may help the efficacy of the process for this confirmation clause to be preceded by a warning such as 'You should only sign this form if you are sure that all the items detailed on it have been fully explained to you.'*

Having a signed confirmation at this stage may provide valuable evidence at any subsequent disciplinary encounter.

3.   *Once signed and completed, the checklist is returned to [personnel administration].*

Induction course

Requiring new recruits to attend an induction course six–eight weeks after they join is also helpful. Such a session held in a quiet, interruption-free room, can provide an opportunity to

- the employer to speak to all newcomers together
- the newcomers to ask their own questions and to hear questions from (and answers given to) those facing similar challenges to their own regarding lack of comprehension of what is required, problems, etc., and
- generate an informal dialogue between both parties on matters of general interest (products, processes, rules, social matters, etc.).

An induction course not only provides an opportunity to check comprehension and awareness of the rules and requirements and to run through any which are not generally understood but also starts the formal communicative process by identifying the actions and attitudes expected of employees.

A formal list of who has attended an induction course, or a note on each employee's file as to when they did so, provides supporting evidence of an opportunity to suggest that the employee must have known what was expected of them should any disciplinary encounter arise.

Informal induction

The foregoing sets out the principles and practice of a structured and formal induction process. However, during every day of most newcomers' first year, there will be information to absorb, procedures to be explained and understood, and guidance to interpret. Advice and support should be provided informally at all times – not simply when a checklist requires it. This is a basic task of management.

Footnote: Few gardeners would plant a shrub or seedling and then leave it to fend for itself. Knowing how difficult it can be for some plants to become established, most conscientious gardeners will tend to check the new item regularly – ensuring it has water, shade or sun as required, is kept free from choking weeds and (if not hardy) protected from frost. Some talk to their plants, and indeed claim that they respond. It is more likely, however, that a plant responds simply since in order to talk to it the gardener has to visit it, and in visiting the essentials (as set out above) for strong growth are likely to be addressed.

So too should it be with newcomers to the organisation, except that, man being a communicative being, most newcomers will welcome the conversation – genuine interest from a manager and the chance to respond could well be the reason for deciding to stay. Many employers report that the highest incidence of labour turnover occurs amongst those that have a year's or less service. If newcomers are left to their own devices it is hardly surprising that they gain misconceptions, make mistakes and feel uninvolved and even unwanted.

International challenges

Introduction

Although it is said that due to the marvels of information technology the world is shrinking fast, examining the problems that are posed when organisations seek to interface with cultures other than their own is an ever-expanding subject which can only be touched upon here. Perhaps the most important point to make is that in dealing with even a close neighbour, considerable research should be undertaken – which itself should be a warning of the degree of research needed when dealing with an entity from a culture remote from and alien to our own. Whilst there are undoubtedly success stories from those who have 'flown by the seat of their pants', there are far many more instances where even leading UK companies have experienced severe problems trying to operate overseas and in many cases have been forced to accept their losses, to 'lick their wounds' and to withdraw from the territory. Indeed often overlooked is the basic problem of senior decision-making management being remote from the operations – the saying 'there is no manure like the farmer's boot' is very apt. Despite apparently sound local management, the fact that those ultimately responsible operate hundreds, even thousands, of miles away, can lead to less effective control than would be the case within the home country – if for no other reason than that visits need to be planned and tend to be stage-managed thus posing a barrier to real two-way communication.

Language

The introduction to this section has deliberately used clichés and expressions which (although such use may have breached good writing guidelines) should be known and accepted by most people in the UK. They may – or may not – be recognised in other English-speaking countries in the world, but it is very unlikely that they will be recognised in non-English speaking countries. Equally those other countries will have similar colloquialisms and sayings of significance to them but holding no real meaning to those not conversant with the intricacies of their language. If communication consists of two parties each understanding what the other means as well as says, then the fact that they speak different languages is crucial. One is reminded of the Rowan Atkinson advertisement where he speaks in a 'native' tongue to a foreigner who responds, also in a native tongue. His sidekick says admiringly 'I didn't realise you were fluent, sir' to which comes the response 'we are both fluent – unfortunately not in the same language'. At least in that encounter the two participants were face to face and if body language and tone account for 93% of the message even gesticulations and facial expressions may suffice in communicating much of what we intend. However, few organisations will wish to leave international interfacing to such a dramatic level of chance.

Interpreters v local agents

The inevitable reaction when two people who do not share a common language wish to do business is for them to find an interpreter who speaks both their native tongues. Obviously the services of an interpreter can assist but even in that instance great care needs to be taken to ensure that the interpreter fully understands the intricacies and nuances connected to the subject matter as well as that of both languages. If the UK exporter is travelling to a foreign country very often it will be the host who provides the interpreter. In that instance the UK exporter could be at a considerable disadvantage in that the interpreter

- may have a bias to the host,
- may not be as fluent in the underlying meanings of English words and phrases that may be used and
- may not understand the significance of some of the more technical aspects of the subject matter.

Despite the expense it may be advisable to commission a UK-based interpreter to accompany the negotiator to ensure the host interpreter correctly interprets what is meant as much as what is said. Conversely it may be safer for the UK exporter to retain an English speaking agent in the foreign country until the language and above all the customs and ways of the host country are fully understood. The additional cost of such a service could be regarded as the price for ensuring reasonable communication.

Attitudes

The background to different races understandably generates different attitudes which pose difficulties particularly when attempting to communicate, and never more so than when attempting to negotiate. If we have an English background we may find a reasonable rapport and understanding with those from the USA, and with other north Europeans. The approach to communication and business in these areas is crisp, businesslike, evidenced by legally binding agreements within a short and productive time-span. However, whilst in the UK particularly the remnants of the 'word is my bond' attitude still prevails, in the USA the buyer is expected to take care of himself and parties may well have swifter recourse to a lawyer. Even in this area the situation is more complex than in the UK where mainly English and to a lesser extent Scottish law are the only codes. In the USA every state has its own interpretation of principles which may be common to most.

The 'let's get on with it' style of the UK and USA is far removed from the more leisurely approach expected in Asia and particularly Japan (where only 1% of the population has ever been outside the country). The concept that there are only a few hours to discuss items is somewhat alien to those societies where often a measured ritual of introductions and pleasantries, even extending to the exchange of small gifts to all present may be expected. Further, any suggestion that business communication or agreements should be evidenced legally may sometimes be viewed as confrontational and unfriendly.

A similarly relaxed style, following a ritualistic procedure, tends to characterise business dealings in countries where the Koran has influence. Personal contacts are all-important – as they are in Latin countries, where again trying to move business forward at too swift a pace may be either counterproductive or carry an expensive price-tag.

Essentially it is necessary to understand, relate to and use the local customs. Attempting to dictate UK customs elsewhere is unlikely to be successful. Generally, in view of the increased globalisation of trade the strictest aspects of old customs may be fading, but it would be unwise to make the assumption that too much progress has been made in this area.

Laws and liabilities

Different countries have different rules of law, and although the UK organisation may attempt to require that any disputes should be dealt with under UK law this may not always be the case. If the host-country legal code is to prevail, a sound understanding of the ramifications will be essential. Again to try to ensure fair treatment it may be advisable to ask legal experts in the UK for a known contact in the other country rather than approaching an indigenous legal operation 'cold'. A full appreciation of all the potential liabilities of doing business in the foreign country is essential – as may be insurance against risks with potentially great exposure.

Customs

Before any type of communication is attempted the customs of the other party need to be assessed and considered. Even in packaging and product colour, there is little one can take for granted since what may be entirely acceptable in the home country could pose severe problems elsewhere.

Checklist: The rainbow problem

Green: In the UK and many Western countries, green is becoming more and more identified with environmentally friendly products (or products claimed to be so) and with 'natural', 'good for you' concepts. This is not, however, true in the Czech Republic and Slovakia where green signifies poison, or in Muslim countries where it tends to be associated with sacred buildings and works of art, whilst in the USA, it is likely to be associated with confectionery.

Red: Again, despite its connotations of danger, this colour provokes no adverse reactions in the UK or most European countries, some of which regard it as a sign of masculinity and strength. In China and Hong Kong it represents happiness and joy, but in Zambia it tends to be associated with thunder and lightning and thus retains these aggressive connotations.

Yellow: Is fairly well accepted throughout the world without too many problems, being regarded in the East as a sign of plenty. In Switzerland yellow tends to be associated with the cosmetic trade and in the USA with homecoming – particularly of the Armed Forces but also of those released from imprisonment (the 'yellow ribbon round the tree' tradition).

Black: May be regarded by many as being smart and attractive although in many countries it is associated with suffering and death. This, however, is not so in China and Hong Kong where it is white that is the colour of mourning.

Pink: To many in the West, being the colour most closely resembling their skin pigment, pink has connotations of cleanliness. However, in the East when used in combination with yellow, pink suggests pornography (usually in the West associated with blue, ironically used by Western detergent manufacturers to suggest cleanliness!).

Note: *The above have been reported as indications of attitudes but attitudes are constantly changing. Many countries in the West (and indeed elsewhere) are becoming increasingly cosmopolitan, which could have the effect of changing their established customs. But this is a slow process which will not occur everywhere. Basically in attempting to interface with those from countries other than our own we cannot afford to assume or to take anything for granted. Research and analysis is essential.*

Response

Inevitably once a market or relationship has been established in a foreign country the home-base office must expect to receive communication from that country. Where this is written it may pose few problems as translators can be commissioned to convert all written items into English and to translate English replies into the other language (replying in English is to be advised only as a means of ensuring the contact does not repeat the process!). Where, however, the contact is by telephone we need to arrange for some means by which the use of the foreign language can be accommodated. Dual-language telephone operators can assist as can the use of a switchboard which indicates the country from which the call emanates, so enabling a response to be made to the caller in his/her own language. This attention to detail and consideration can be an impressive form of communication in its own right.

Translation problems

English is a 'short' language. If it is decided to translate a piece of English into another language it will normally occupy around 10–15% more space on the page in the foreign language than it does in English. To ensure that the true message has been preserved, it may be helpful once the English has been translated into the foreign language to ask a different translator to translate the foreign-language version back into English. Comparison of the original and the doubly-translated copy may provide surprises.

Additional Reference: See data available from foreign embassies and consulates, plus the *Economist* Business Travellers Guides.

Interviewing

Introduction

The interview scenario is used in a variety of contexts – job application, negotiation, to collect data for a report, etc. Many principles apply in all situations and since the application interview is the most common it may be appropriate to use that as the template. To an applicant, the job interview is the first main communication exercise to which they will be exposed with their potential employer. Accordingly consideration should be given to the manner in which such a meeting is arranged, the reception given to the applicant and the way in which the interview is conducted. The key to all effective and successful interviews is preparation (by both parties) and an understanding, particularly on the part of the prospective employer, that in addition to their wish and need to obtain information from the applicant to decide whether he or she is suitable for their requirements, equally the applicant needs to have information to make a decision to join or not. Too often this duality of interest is not fully appreciated.

Preparation

The checklist below (p. 194) offers advice concerning the logistics of the interview, and it cannot be stressed too strongly how important it is for the interviewer to set aside sufficient time for a proper two-way discussion and, above all, to protect the session from interruption. Interruptions caused by telephone calls or visitors are not only basic bad manners but also they stop the natural flow of the interview and convey totally the wrong impression to the interviewee. Some messages need no words, and breaking off an interview to deal with a telephone call or intruder sends the interviewee a semiotic message – 'you (or my contact with you) are not as important as this other matter with which I must deal'. Whilst this may in fact be the case, it is hardly a satisfactory initial message for a potential employee.

Thus interviewers should at the very least ensure that sufficient uninterrupted time is allowed for the interview.

Similar unfortunate messages are conveyed when it is obvious that the interviewer cannot remember the name of the interviewee or has only the vaguest memory of their experience and/or qualifications, etc.

Thus attention needs to be paid to the following points:

(a) Learning (virtually verbatim if possible):

- the requirements of the vacancy (using a job description/person specification, as well as any personal knowledge)
- details of any interpersonal skills required
- the minimum experience, training and expertise needed, and personal characteristics preferred, of the ideal candidate.

(b) Finding out as much about the candidate as the application form and/or letter of application (or covering letter) allow.

This 'instant recall' knowledge should avoid the need to refer to the paperwork during the interview to check facts – at the least a search to check a reference will break the flow of the interview. In addition, knowing what is required, and what is on offer from a particular candidate should automatically reveal apparent gaps in knowledge which can be checked.

(c) Make notes of items contained in the application which require amplification and/or explanation, particularly of reasons for leaving previous positions (especially if previous employment periods tend to be short).

(d) Prepare questions that will check the depth and range of knowledge on subjects which are essential for the job on offer – i.e. open questions that cannot be answered 'yes' or 'no' (see item 5 in the following checklist). This may entail research on the part of the interviewer so that s/he can talk knowledgeably on the subject in order to 'pump prime' the discussion.

Checklist: Running the interview

1. A set time should be allowed for the interview and, assuming the interviewee is present, the interview should start promptly. If, due to unavoidable circumstances, delay is caused by the interviewer, an apology should be made and the situation updated at least every five minutes.
2. A quiet room (unplug the telephone) should be used. Ideally interruption should always be avoided, but if this is impossible the situation should be explained to the interviewee, an apology offered and the interruption minimised. If the interruption lasts longer than

five minutes updates should be given then and at least every further five minutes.

Note: *In the event of lengthy delay or interruption, as well as an apology being provided, the interviewee should be given the opportunity to arrange an alternative time. Costs involved should be reimbursed.*

3. The parties should be seated at the same height and in comfortable chairs, and not under strong lights, as they tend to dazzle.

4. The interviewer should spend a few minutes on introductory matters attempting to place the applicant at their ease. It might be appropriate to take the initiative and outline some history of the organisation, its products and status in the marketplace.

5. The bulk of the interview time should be spent obtaining information concerning the career and experience, etc., of the applicant and providing information regarding the position, requirements and prospects of the job. In this regard it is essential to use open questions ('tell me about', 'how did you cope with . . . ?' 'what was best (and worst) about . . . ?'), and so on, rather than closed questions ('did you enjoy . . . ?', 'you didn't stay there long did you . . . ?'). This should ensure that the interviewee has to answer with sentences and comments rather than simply saying 'yes' or 'no'. It is also essential that the interviewer is seen to 'listen' and to be attentive. Taking notes may be one way of indicating this, whereas thumbing through the papers whilst not looking at the interviewee is not – it can indicate to the interviewee a lack of interest in the answer being provided. Control of such 'body language' is essential since powerful messages are sent in this way. If the interviewee gains the impression that the interviewer is not interested they are unlikely to give of their best.

6. Where possible, check the technical expertise claimed by the interviewee. The impression should not be given that the interviewer is expert in the subject (unless, of course he is, and even then it might be better to conceal such knowledge and let the applicant speak). It may help the applicant to talk if the conversation is kept going with such comments as 'I don't know much about this, but I thought that . . .'. Such gambits allow the applicant free rein to explain the point, or if the opportunity is declined, it may indicate that experience is not as wide or applicable as was previously thought.

7. Guide the conversation to the preferred route with the minimum of intervention, so that the applicant is encouraged to talk at length. During this, the applicant's knowledge can be better displayed and better tested. This part of the interview should take the form of a discussion about the vacancy and the applicant's suitability for it. It should be objective and attempt to avoid any judgemental overtones –

talents and experience vary from person to person. An interview should not be an assessment of whether the applicant is 'up to the job', but whether the requirements of the organisation and the attributes and attitude, skills and experience of the applicant represent a match with such requirements.

8. For certain vacancies (e.g. recruiting assemblers, word-processing operators, etc.) where technical skills are essential, it may be appropriate to arrange a short 'hands-on' test.

9. Every opportunity should be afforded to the interviewee for them to ask questions on any topic related to [the organisation], vacancy, prospects, etc.

Concluding the interview

Interviews should conclude naturally at the point where both parties feel that they have as much information about the other sufficient for their purposes. For most positions this is unlikely to be less than 30 minutes after the start of the interview, and for supervisory and more senior positions, less than 60 minutes, bearing in mind that in recruiting for such positions it will be normal to invite applicants for a second (and further) interview(s).

At the end the interviewer should state the position regarding the recruitment. This could be that

(a) the applicant is not suitable to be considered further – in which case they should be told so immediately.

(b) a short list is being prepared, and any short-listed applicant will be required to attend for further interview. Usually there will be a need for the interviewee to be contacted at a later date with the decision. If so, then a date should be given. It is essential, having given such a date, that it is adhered to (even if the call is only to further defer the date/decision).

(c) the applicant is required to return for further interview possibly by another interviewer. Again, if possible a date should be set.

(d) a decision will be made within a set time and the interviewee will be contacted. Again whatever date is given should be adhered to.

(e) the interviewee is entirely suitable and is to be offered the position.

Assessment and follow up

Immediately after the interview, the interviewer should make an assessment of the interviewee. Where there are several applicants, an interview assessment form should be completed to facilitate ease of comparison between them. Once a decision is made, then all applicants should be advised of the outcome promptly, with the successful applicant being sent an offer letter and, once an indication of acceptance has been received, a full information pack on the employer (thus starting the communication process outlined in INDUCTION).

Unsuccessful applicants should feel that they have been fairly treated, that they have had an objective interview and that they knew enough of the employer to have made a decision had the job been offered to them.

Tailpiece

The advent of technology is causing reconsideration of the methods of applicant interviewing. An increasing number of organisations are using telephone interviews at least as a first stage in the process for more senior appointments. Applicants surveyed seem, however, to give less good accounts of themselves when being interviewed over the phone. It has been suggested that this is because being at home they are dressed and posed informally and have not adopted the 'professional' approach they would in the interviewer's office. Virtually simultaneously a product has been developed that enables a caller to tell whether the other party is telling the truth or not. This could be of considerable assistance, bearing in mind a substantial proportion of applicants do lie during job interviews.

Finally, in the USA increasingly organisations are using their WEB SITE to display details of the job and career opportunities they have available to all site visitors. Job seekers, particularly those at university, can access the web site of the organisation via the university's computer and because that part of the site is interactive, can 'complete' a job application form and await further contact by the organisation.

Joint consultation

Introduction

Employees are more likely to be able to achieve what is required of them if they understand what their employer is attempting. Whilst with smaller organisations this communication requirement should be relatively easy to satisfy (although a 1995 survey indicated that in general smaller organisations tended to be regarded as poorer communicators than their larger counterparts) the larger the organisation the more difficult this may be to achieve particularly on a personal dialogue basis. However, such dialogue may be possible with representatives of larger workforces, and one forum for providing such an exchange of information is a Joint Consultative Committee consisting of representatives of both management and workforce, meeting regularly to consider both items included within a constitution and other matters which might arise from time to time.

Implementation

The following résumé covers the policy, procedural and constitutional aspects of operating a JCC.

Checklist: Control and operation of a JCC

Purpose of a Joint Consultative Committee (JCC)
1. Our overall object is to assist everyone in understanding and achieving the organisational aims effectively and efficiently.
2. The object of joint consultation is to provide an opportunity for management and employees to discuss matters of common interest which will help both parties attain their aims. In particular, they would need to consult each other, and to consider each other's requirements and interests – preferably before decisions are made.
3. The JCC will consist of an equal number of representatives – half elected by employees and half appointed by management.

4. The JCC can discuss problems and suggest solutions. It can make recommendations or state preferences for or against certain decisions. It cannot make decisions.

5. Elected representatives will be allowed such time as is reasonable to carry out their duties. These duties will include:

   - canvassing their constituents for items for consideration at forthcoming JCC meetings
   - conducting such research as may be necessary to brief themselves on matters for discussion by the JCC
   - reporting back to their constituents, and
   - advising the following JCC meeting of feedback, etc.

6. Any JCC member may request any item be considered at a JCC meeting other than matters relating to an individual (which should be raised individually under the grievance procedure).

7. Full discussion will be allowed of each item raised at a JCC meeting and details of the item, the discussion and any recommendation made will be minuted.

8. The minutes of each JCC meeting will be posted on the notice boards and given to each JCC member and manager. Each elected JCC member will also receive a number of copies for use within their constituency. Decisions on matters raised for management consideration will be made as soon as possible and reported on at the following JCC meeting.

9. All elected JCC members should have a deputy or alternate who can attend meetings in their place.

Constitution

1. *Purpose*
   - to promote the fullest use of the accumulated knowledge, experience, skills and ideas of employees in the efficient running of the organisation
   - to give employees a voice in decisions that affect them, and a chance to affect such decisions
   - to enable management to gain the views of employees and to take account of such views in planning
   - to avoid conflict by giving management and employees the opportunity to listen to and reach an understanding of each other's views and objectives
   - to provide elected representatives with which [the organisation] can consult in the event of redundancy.

2. *Organisation*
- A committee consisting of [number] employee representatives and [equal number] management representatives meeting [every other month] to consider an agenda of items submitted by its members (who will have canvassed their constituents for such items) and/or management.
- The senior management representative will act as chairman, whilst a deputy chairman will be selected from the elected representatives. The [personnel administrator] will act as the non-voting secretary.
- The committee may consider all [organisation-related] subjects (other than trade secrets, confidential information and an individual or his/her details). It is expected that the JCC will consider matters relating to

  - the efficiency and productivity of [the organisation]
  - the methods, conditions and procedures of work and of any changes thereto
  - personnel polices and procedures
  - appraisal, training and education
  - organisation rules and policies
  - health and safety matters
  - social and community-related matters.

- An agenda will be issued at least five working days before every meeting to all members, and minutes will be issued within five working days of the meeting to all members, the notice boards, and all managers. Elected representatives will have additional copies of minutes for use in their constituencies.
- Elected representatives will be provided with administrative support and stationery, and will be allowed reasonable time away from their job to carry out their duties, which will include obtaining input from their constituents regarding matters to be raised at a JCC meeting, research on matters on the agenda, attending meetings and reporting back to their constituents.

Rules

1. Consultation will take place by means of committee meetings which will be held [monthly, two monthly, quarterly, etc.]
2. The constituencies will be . . .

> *Note:* It is unlikely that a JCC representative could operate effectively with a constituency in excess of 60/75 employees. This predetermines the number of representatives and, since the representatives should ideally be matched by the number of management nominees, the size of the committee. The workplace needs to be divided into constituencies roughly equal in size. To avoid waste of the representatives' time, the departments forming a constituency should be adjacent or work-linked. Very large departments may need to be allocated more than one representative.

3. Any employee working within the constituency may be nominated for election as a representative. Nomination must be on a form to be provided and must be supported by the signatures of [five] other employees working within the constituency. Nominations must be handed to the [secretary] at least five days in advance of the date set for the election, which will take place during [month] each year. The list of candidates seeking election in a constituency will be posted on all notice boards within the constituency at least two clear days before the election. If only one nomination is received the employee nominated will automatically be declared elected without an election. If an election is necessary, all employees within the constituency will be given a voting form by the [specify], and those employees will be able to vote in accordance with the rules laid down at the time. The [secretary] and two management representatives will be responsible for counting the votes cast. In the event of a tie, the tied candidates will be required to toss a coin to decide who is to be the representative, and the losing candidate (or the candidate coming second where there is no tie) will automatically become the deputy, or alternate, for that constituency.

4. Members will hold office for a maximum of [three] consecutive years. Having left the committee for a year, after completion of a [three-] year term, an employee can rejoin the committee, if elected or appointed by management. At the end of each year, [two] management representatives and [two] elected representatives will retire. Those who retire in the first [two] years will be selected by ballot, thereafter whoever has served longest will retire. All persons retiring may seek re-election, provided this would not breach the [three] consecutive years' service limit.

5. Elected representatives will be expected to serve the interests of their constituents – keeping them informed and endeavouring to ensure their views are made known at JCC meetings.

6. Amendment to the constitution may be effected by the organisation, following consultation with the JCC.

Journals and newsletters

Introduction

Research indicates that in terms of receiving information and participating in a communication process, employee preference (in order of priority) is

- face-to-face conversation
- informal briefing by team leader (see BRIEFING)
- formal briefing by senior management, and, lastly,
- written information.

Whilst there can be no adequate substitute for genuinely motivated face-to-face communication between employer and employee to foster a better understanding of what is required, to create a better working environment and to engender a better team spirit, time constraints often dictate that written information must be employed as a substitute.

Basis

The production of an organisation's own newsletter or journal, particularly if business news is restricted to no more than 25–30% and employees are encouraged to write for the journal themselves, can be a very valuable means of underpinning and supporting the communication aims, particularly where an organisation operates through a large number of geographically remote units.

The most effective newsletters and journals are those that

- restrict business news as suggested above
- use an informal user-friendly style and presentation
- feature people and personal news
- are presented in an attractive and easy-to-read format
- use illustrations and colour and, above all,
- invite employees to contribute to the content so that they come to 'own' and identify with the item.

Checklist: Production of journal/newsletter

1. [The organisation] will publish its own [newsletter/journal] which will be entitled [specify] and will be edited by [specify]. It will be produced [number] times each year on [publication dates].

2. Its purposes are to

   (a) provide information to and encourage the generation of a two-way communication channel between

   - organisation and employees,
   - employee and organisation, and
   - employee and employee.

   (In this context 'employees' includes active and retired personnel and their relatives and dependants.)

   (b) provide information on company, personnel and personal activities, product sales and launches performance, industry activities and so on

   (c) provide information on and comprehension of the financial results of [the organisation]

   (d) help create a rapport amongst those working in and concerned with [the organisation]

   (e) help improve the commitment of the employees to the aims of [the organisation].

3. The journal will be produced primarily for the active employees of [the organisation], but should also seek to satisfy the requirements of retired employees, shareholders, suppliers and customers.

4. Since the journal may be read by competitors it is necessary to exercise some discretion when featuring reports on confidential aspects of new products, financial results, processes, etc.

5. Since the journal will be read outside [the organisation] – even if this may not be the intent – it is expected that its presentation, style and content should be of such a standard that it will not detract from the reputation or standing of [the organisation].

6. The Board does not wish there to be any censorship of items included but does expect the editor to try to maintain an acceptable standard of English and content, and to avoid giving offence to any reader or section of readers in keeping with the ethos of [the organisation].

7. The journal may deal with all matters arising from the activities of [the organisation], except those relating to an individual's pay and/or benefits, contract terms, personal details and/or life, unless they have so authorised agreement in writing in advance.

8. The editor and the journal will be bound by the confidential agreement applicable to all directors and staff regarding the issue and use of price-sensitive information.

9. The journal should avoid making criticisms of any internal or external person or body unless that body is given a right of reply. Any such reply should appear adjacent to the criticisms, in the same issue and enjoy commensurate space and position. Anonymous letters or articles [may be/are not to be] featured.

10. If the editor is unsure whether to include a particular article he/she should refer to [specify] for guidance.

11. The editor will have complete discretion (subject to this statement) regarding content and presentation, but will endeavour at all times to ensure the journal satisfies its aims as set out above, particularly (d) and (e).

12. The editor will be responsible for compiling and submitting a budget to [specify] and for adhering to that budget. Special features such as the [History of the Company and the celebration of the company's nth anniversary] which are to be featured in the journal will be subject to a supplementary budget to be agreed separately.

13. The budget will need to reflect external sourcing of all design, illustrating and printing facilities. The editor will have the use of word processing facilities in the [name] department.

Contributions

If the newsletter is intended to work as a two-way communication channel, this will only occur if the editor actively encourages as many employees as possible to contribute. Whilst this can give rise to problems of content and quality, care must be taken not to discourage any reader from becoming a writer as the more employees who can be encouraged to write for the journal, the more proprietorial will be their attitude towards it, and the greater their commitment to both the paper and its sponsoring organisation.

A correspondents' brief is a useful guide for would-be contributors, and will help to provide quality copy.

Example: Correspondents' brief

1. Copy for [name] is required by the copy dates which are [dates].

2. Copy is ideally submitted typed double-spaced (i.e. written on every other line) on one side of A4 paper, but handwritten copy will be accepted

provided it is clearly written (again double-spaced and on one side of the paper). There is no need to worry about grammar and spelling as this will be automatically corrected.

3. Authors should try at all times to be accurate and to provide full details of all items included in the copy. For example, dates, places, names (forenames and surnames), locations, departments, etc., should be included (in capitals, if the copy is handwritten) to avoid misspellings.

4. The editor will normally indicate the number of words required, except in the case of articles written on a purely 'speculative' basis. It can be difficult to write to a set number of words but every effort should be made to keep to any wordage required as this indicates that space has been allocated for the article. Articles submitted which exceed the number of words required may need to be edited.

5. The article should bear a suitable title although the editor reserves the right to change this or to substitute another.

6. The style of [name] is such that we require 'bite'-sized pieces of text. Articles should be broken up into paragraphs of no more than [number of words – which will depend on the size of type, layout, number of columns, etc.] with each introduced by a heading, quotation or wording which either leads into the following paragraph or indicates its content. The purpose of this requirement is to ensure the overall presentation of the journal is enticing throughout.

7. Our style is relaxed and articles should be written in this way. Try to avoid using jargon or, if it is inevitable, explain it. Try to vary the words used – especially verbs – as this will aid the appeal of the piece. However, don't use unusual words just for the sake of it.

8. All articles make a greater impact if they are supported by an illustration (photo, drawing, cartoon, etc.). In writing your article try to think of suitable illustrations that could form part of the finished item. If you can provide your own illustration please send it with the article – it can be returned if a self-addressed envelope is included. A note of the name and address of the sender should be attached to the photo using detachable stickers. The rear of a photo should not be written upon. (See checklist below for guidance on taking photographs.)

9. Copy and illustrations are submitted to the editor on the understanding that this is a voluntary and unpaid system, and that the item is the work of the person submitting the copy. If this is not the case it should be made clear on the item, and, if appropriate, the agreement of the author

obtained to the inclusion of the item. No guarantee of inclusion can be given either for the issue for which the item is submitted or for any subsequent issues for which it may be held over.

10. The correspondents acting for the editor are as follows: (names and departments) and they will act as postboxes and provide local/immediate assistance. To save time the correspondents may check articles as they are handed in, and may request further information in order to ensure each item is complete before passing it to the editor.

11. In the event of a complaint being made, the person or organisation against whom the complaint is made will always be given a right of reply in the same issue as the complaint appears. This may mean delaying inclusion pending receipt of the reply.

12. The editor's decision regarding inclusion and/or editing of any article will be final, and no correspondence regarding such decisions can be entered into.

Checklist: Guidance for photographers

1. Avoid the stereotyped poses – handshakes on leaving, promotion, etc., signing the contract, making a phone call or (above all) the 'grip 'n' grins passing-out pose' complete with everyone shaking hands and holding a certificate. Try for some originality.

2. Smile naturally – but that is far easier said than done. So catch people unawares – and take plenty of shots on the offchance that one or more will be of good quality.

3. Avoid the mesmerised-rabbit shot – caught in the headlights' beam. (Catching people unawares may avoid this.) If posing subjects, suggest they do look not straight at the camera but at the top of the photographer's head (this will minimise the 'red-eye' effect, although many modern cameras can now avoid this). Try to relax subjects and give them something to do with their hands (not clasping them in front of them or folding their arms).

4. If the photographer stands slightly above the target and to one side, not only will this help minimise double-chins, shadows and elongated noses but it will accentuate cheek-bones and give greater depth to a face photo. Taking a shot from this angle will also make the subjects look slightly thinner.

5. Avoid the Dorian Grey concept. Photographs are ideal for capturing history – but don't let anyone keep submitting the same photo year after year.

6. Linking people with product (and even with customers) can be a great concept as long as it looks natural. If you have to pose the shot it may look artificial, so give the pose some thought.

7. Give people time to compose themselves, and take a number of shots – possibly some *while* they are composing themselves – then one might be more natural. Have a mirror available so that hair, makeup, ties and jackets can be checked for neatness. Those who wear glasses but do not want to be photographed wearing them should be given time for any 'nose marks' to disappear. Make sure that lights do not reflect off bald heads or foreheads. If necessary powder such shiny spots.

8. Check that jackets, blouses, collars and dresses are lying properly. No-one will thank you for a photo that makes them look foolish. If this happens they may resist being photographed again.

9. If people are sitting try to get the camera slightly above their level of vision, so they look up – this is preferable to them looking down, which can be very unflattering.

10. With non-people photos make sure the subject matter is interesting. (How fascinating is that building?)

11. Keep a look out for the odd angles. Be original – don't do what everyone else does. It may not come off but at least it will be original!

12. Above all, don't forget: a picture is worth a thousand words.

Meetings

Introduction

A meeting, if well conducted, can be a good means of communication as well as the decision-making forum which is its prime aim. Cynics have said that meetings take minutes and waste hours, and there is no doubt that unless run effectively and with purpose this can be all too true. There is a danger not only of holding meetings for 'meetings' sake', but also of using the incidence of meetings to defer decision-making by a manager in favour of the collective voice.

Main principles

If it is felt that meetings are not effective, then it is almost certainly because the organisation, and particularly the chairman, has not

- considered the reason for the meeting sufficiently,
- set its purpose within the right context, and/or
- made sufficient effort to control the meeting (and individual members) so that it achieves this purpose.

It has been suggested that no meeting should last much longer than two–three hours. If it does, unless the subject matter is especially focused there is a danger that attentiveness will wane. Ideally the chairman should set the expected duration of the meeting at its beginning and, working within the time span so set, endeavour to give each item of business a rough allocation of time – pushing members to come to a decision and move on. Some meeting members can be tempted to 'justify their presence' by long-winded comments which often contain little of value.

Agenda

Inevitably the construction of an agenda will depend very much on the type of meeting required – but equally the efficiency of the meeting can depend how constructively the agenda is compiled. If it is a regular monitoring meeting it could comprise items drawn from the following sources

(a) an annual list of items
(b) items to be considered or reconsidered requested from the previous or an earlier meeting
(c) new business arising since the previous meeting out of the operation of the organisation
(d) items requested to be considered by members (individual house rules may apply to these items – e.g. they may be required to be approved by the chairman for inclusion)
(e) regular reports (accounts, cash forecast, contracts, etc.)
(f) market, economic or legal changes affecting the business
(g) statutorily (or similarly) required items (e.g. for a company – approval of the report of the directors and annual accounts for submission to the AGM, dividend recommendation, etc.).

Alternatively a meeting may be required to consider a particular (and thus sole) subject. In this case there is greater scope for determining the extent of the deliberations, the aim and the duration by generating what can be called a 'dynamic agenda'.

Example: Dynamic agenda

AGENDA
for an [informal executive] meeting to be held on
[date one week ahead]
in the Company Boardroom at 2p.m. prompt

Subject: Absenteeism

Aims of meeting: To devise and implement [up to five] tactics or initiatives for immediate implementation to reduce absenteeism to near or below the industry average.

Purpose of discussion:
1. To consider monthly reports of staff absenteeism over past 12 months (see analysis attached).

2. To compare such reports with analyses of absenteeism throughout the industry (see report from [Industry] Trade Association attached).

3. To consider whether there are special reasons for this company's poor performance, and if so what can be changed / improved to ensure a reduction.

4. To determine [five or more] methods to ensure such a reduction. Members will be expected to attend with ideas for consideration at the meeting, such ideas must be capable of implementation within 14 days.

Administration: The meeting duration will be two hours.
No interruptions or messages.

Attendance: Personnel Manager, Company Nurse,
Company Secretary, Works Manager,
Sales Manager

Notes:
(a) Setting the meeting a week ahead should allow ample thinking time.

(b) Providing internal statistics with external comparisons sets the problem in context with the delay before the meeting allowing time for assimilation of the data.

(c) Requesting members' ideas should assist accountability.

(d) Stating that there must be no interruptions not only allows meeting members to brief their staff accordingly but also underlines the importance attached to the subject by the chairman. It is not unknown for some meeting attenders to arrange for deliberate interruptions to meetings either to enable them to escape some agenda items or simply to try to bolster their own importance.

(e) The tone and structure of the agenda itself seeks to demonstrate that action is required. It implies an urgency reflecting that of the subject.

With regular meetings an agenda should always follow a set format and order, whilst the grouping of like items under general headings may assist the logical 'flow' of the business of the meeting. Setting out under each item the aim of the business (for example a draft resolution) should help concentrate the mind on what needs to be addressed.

Timing

Ideally an agenda should be despatched at least seven days prior to the meeting and be accompanied by all relevant documents. Unless this occurs, many members will attend not having read the papers, leading in turn to decisions being taken on incomplete knowledge. In addition, some of the meeting time will be consumed by the need for individuals to check points in documents only received just before or even at the meeting. Where papers do need to be given to members at a late stage a résumé of the salient points should be requested as a covering sheet.

Aims

Meetings exist to take decisions. The chairman/meeting should establish what decisions are required and by when. These should be stated when the body is set up (e.g. as its terms of reference) and possibly repeated at the beginning of the meeting to encourage focusing of attention. Where use is made of a dynamic agenda this principle can be reflected within the agenda itself.

Composition and cost

Only those required to attend should do so, since a meeting's length can be proportionate to the number present. If that number is swelled by persons whose contribution is unnecessary, the effectiveness of those required to be present and of the meeting as a whole will be diluted. Unfortunately attendance at a meeting can sometimes be regarded as an indicator of importance and become an enticement to attend even when there is no point.

Calculating the cost per minute of those present taking part in the meeting (based on annual salary plus oncosts) may encourage a crude cost-benefit analysis of the value of the decisions reached. Consideration of such cost may concentrate the mind on who should be present. All members should be encouraged to make effective contributions that are concise yet comprehensive.

Data

Reports, analyses and all other data required for consideration by the meeting should accompany the agenda, or a note regarding late submission be appended thereto. Tabling a bulky or complex report should be avoided as decision-taking on its contents is likely to be uninformed. Where such data comprises bulky or complex reports, an accompanying précis of findings and/or recommendations may be useful. A rule that all reports should contain brief and prioritised recommendations may encourage effective analysis and action. Data enclosures should be assembled in agenda order.

Minutes

(a) *Taking:* Minutes of the meeting should be taken by the Secretary or deputy and should contain a résumé of the decisions taken – not necessarily the reasons for the decisions.

Note: *Minutes usually record decisions but if they are required to be used as an information tool the meeting may decide that reasons for decisions are incorporated.*

Whether they are decision-records or information-disseminators, the minutes must be an accurate record. This is particularly important if the organisation needs to produce a certified copy of a minute to a third party, e.g. to evidence a signatory's authority to negotiate and agree a contract. If notes were taken at the meeting from which the minutes were composed it may be wise, once the minutes have been approved, to destroy such notes. The minutes as approved are the record of the meeting – having (possibly) contradictory notes available could be embarrassing in the event of a challenge to the veracity of the minutes.

(b) *Content:* This varies according to the custom of the organisation and/or the preference of the chairman, but generally minutes should be full enough and contain sufficient information, to enable a third party to be able to comprehend the decisions taken. At times (e.g. if setting up divisional boards comprising newcomers to the role of directors) it may be necessary to include additional explanations.

(c) *Approval:* The minutes should be prepared as soon as possible after the conclusion of the meeting and approved in principle by the chairman. Whether such approved draft minutes are sent immediately to all members (or held to accompany the agenda for the next meeting) is for the meeting to decide, although if using them as action-prompts the former is essential. Approval of the minutes as a true record should be sought from those present, at their next following meeting. As evidence of that approval it is good practice for the chairman of the following meeting to sign the last page of such minutes and to initial all previous pages. The minutes then stand as prima-facie evidence of the decisions of the meeting – they can still be challenged, but this will be difficult if those present have agreed them as a true record.

(d) *Use as action prompts:* Minutes can be used in this way, encouraging accountability and timely action. To achieve this the initials of those responsible should be inserted against each item for action with a note of the date for completion. At the following meeting (or possibly outside the meeting and prior to the following meeting) each person is required to report upon the status of the item for which they were responsible.

e) *Security:* Both original and copy minutes of Board meetings must be kept securely. They can be kept in bound books or, more usually, in lockable loose-leaf binders, in which case all pages should be sequentially numbered and appropriate protection against falsification taken. Minutes of other meetings should also be kept as they are, once approved, a record of what transpired and what decisions were taken.

(f) *Inspection:* Minutes of General Meetings should be kept at the registered office of the company (and must be made available for inspection by shareholders for two hours each working day). There is no restriction on the location of minutes of Board meetings or any other meetings. Generally only directors have a right of inspection of Board-meeting minutes, although auditors will normally request inspection or copies to evidence decisions affecting accounts, etc.

(g) *Index:* Minutes should always be indexed and cross-referenced to aid swift reference back to previous decisions.

(h) *Dissension:* In the event of one or more members opposing the decision ultimately taken, the dissenters can request that a note of such dissension is recorded in the minutes.

(i) *Alteration:* Since they are intended to be a true record of decisions taken, in the event of any error in the minutes either the record copy should be altered and the chairman should initial the alteration, or a new version should be prepared, issued, approved and signed.

(j) *Approval:* The best practice is for the approval of the minutes of the previous meeting to be the first main item on the agenda of the following meeting and for the chairman of that subsequent meeting, with the approval of those present who were present at the previous meeting, to sign and date the minutes.

Procedure

Although the level of formality of the meeting will differ widely according to individual company preferences and custom, it is usual for all members to sign a book of attendance, and to address and speak through the chairman, and for the chairman to summarise the decision(s), before taking the 'sense' or decision of the meeting – usually by consensus, but occasionally by vote. Summarising the decision aids the accurate preparation of the minutes. In a Board meeting each person entitled to be present has a right to be heard on each subject, since the authority for the decisions depends on the collective responsibility of the Board as an entity. Ground rules may need to be set for procedure at other meetings.

Quorum

If a quorum is required under the terms of reference (which should be checked), the secretary should ensure these requirements can be met. If regular difficulty is experienced obtaining a quorum, the terms of reference (even articles) should be considered for review.

Timetable

For regular meetings (e.g. for a Board of Directors) certain business usually needs to be transacted at set times of the year. The secretary should publish a list of meetings dates for at least a year ahead. This could include firm dates for (say) nine months, with suggested dates for later meetings which would be confirmed by an updated timetable issued on (say) a rolling six-monthly basis. This list should incorporate reference to such business, e.g. dividend payment, preliminary announcement and report publication dates, etc. (where applicable).

Voting

Whilst often business is agreed by consensus, there will be occasions when a formal vote needs to be taken. The voting power of individual members needs to be checked against the terms of reference/appointment. Whether the chairman has a second or casting vote (or even any vote) should be checked.

Mentoring

Introduction

The highest labour turnover in many organisations occurs amongst those with less than one year's service. Often the failure to convert a recruit into a longer-term employee is entirely due to the organisation not arranging the INDUCTION (in the widest sense of the word) of newcomers adequately. Given the costs of recruitment this can mean a considerable wastage of resources. One means of assisting newcomers to settle down is by the use of mentors. The essential characteristics of a mentor are

- the ability to watch a recruit or newcomer discreetly, and

- to be on hand to answer questions or concerns and provide guidance with both information and advice on 'the way things are done around here' and on career considerations. Realistically, a more established employee may be able to raise potential concerns at a higher level than would be immediately available to a new employee.

Administration and training

Those who are to act as mentors need to understand the aims and objectives of the scheme, to be trained in dealing with the problems that employees in their 'care' will tend to experience, and be allowed time away from their own duties to provide such a service. They may also need training

- in how to provide support and assistance in a tactful manner
- to appreciate that the chain of command needs to be preserved between recruit and immediate superior and
- to ensure they realise that their role is provide personal assistance and guidance rather than instruction.

Mentors need to be given authority commensurate with their duties – for example ideally they should be able to communicate with a newcomer's line supervisor regarding problems that are occurring, perhaps only in an informing and advisory capacity, but nevertheless as equals.

Checklist: Principles and practice of mentoring

1. An organisation needs to determine the aims and objectives of the scheme (e.g. to provide a service for newcomers that will help them assimilate requirements placed upon them and speedily become absorbed into the life of the organisation).

2. A decision needs to be made regarding who is to be covered. For instance, is the scheme aimed at a particular intake of employee (e.g. graduates), or a section of the workforce seen to be disadvantaged (e.g. female or ethnic-minority employees), or those who are suffering particular problems due to workplace changes (e.g. operators required to learn a new computerised system)?

3. A senior manager must be appointed to oversee the whole scheme – including the determination of disputes that may be generated through the operation of the scheme, etc.

4. It needs to be decided whether the scheme is to be compulsory or voluntary. A voluntary scheme may be preferable since some managers may wish to provide such a service themselves and could resent the 'imposition' of another party into the relationship with their employees.

5. The aim and purpose of the scheme needs to be communicated to all involved, stressing that mentors are available to help and to work with line managers, not to be a substitute for them. Suggestions made by mentors need to be relayed to managers who can then act on them and take the necessary action.

6. It may be helpful to operate a pilot scheme with volunteers, and to survey every aspect – altering arrangements as necessary in the light of experience.

7. The scheme's operation should be reviewed after six months, surveying the feelings of newcomers, mentors and line managers, and alterations made as a result of such feedback.

Induction

A valuable aspect of the duties of a mentor is ensuring that the employee knows and understands what is expected of him/her. Thus one could expect a mentor to play a leading part in overseeing the INDUCTION of a new employee, providing discreet guidance on rules, regulations, etc., being available should there be problems of comprehension of job descriptions, and so on.

Organisation charts

Introduction

For a newcomer to an organisation or a supplier working with the organisation for the first time, the relationships between various departments can be difficult to understand. One of the most effective ways of demonstrating such relationships is diagrammatically. Representing departments by boxes and their interconnection by lines may provide guidance to such interfacing far more easily than any specification or word description. Often such knowledge may be essential in comprehending priorities and procedures, particularly for those at a non-managerial level. Taking this one stage further, departmental relationship charts may also assist in putting everything into perspective – literally.

Examples

In the two examples shown below the same structure has been depicted. The 'vertical levels of authority' is widely used but suffers from two drawbacks. It is usually shown (as here) as a pyramid, with the chairman/chief executive at the 'top' and the ordinary employees at the 'bottom', which may emphasise the subservient role of the majority of employees – an inference which may be against the ethos of the organisation. This can be overcome by simply inverting the pyramid – the relationships do not alter, but the psychological overtones of being at the 'top' and 'bottom' are at least blurred. The other disadvantage is that being drawn in vertical levels it implies that departments (and their managers) or personnel on the same level, have the same 'importance' or 'value'. Logically, it may be preferable to show the departments on different levels to emphasise a relationship, even though their status may be identical. Either the relative positions of departments and/or personnel should be carefully checked and discrepancies eradicated or the chart should carry a note such as 'The positioning of departments on certain levels is not indicative of importance, status or responsibility.' Even with such a warning it is difficult to overcome the strong inference of 'equality' (or 'inequality') presented by the visual image of the chart.

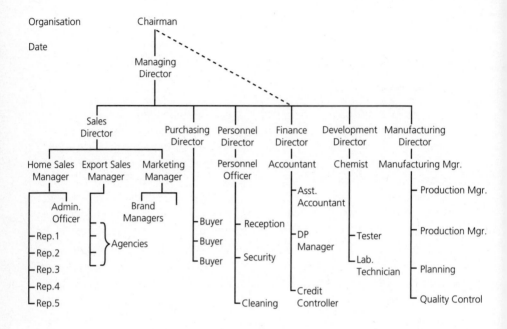

Note: Levels are not indicative of seniority.

Departmental chart

As an alternative, the chart can be drawn with departments depicted within circles emanating from the Board, which is shown as the core (see over). This overcomes the 'top' and 'bottom' overtones and blurs the problem that may arise over levels of importance and/or authority. However, it also blurs the chain of command and does not show the relationships between departments clearly.

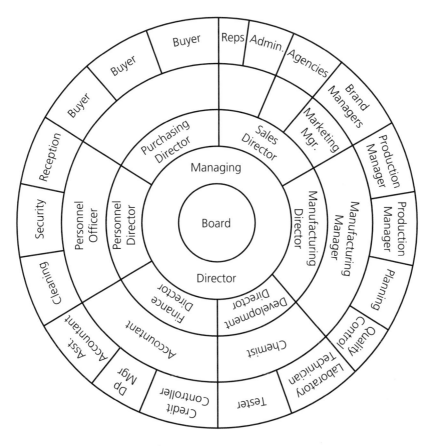

Note: Levels are not indicative of seniority.

Circular departmental chart

Relationship charts

Organisation charts tend, as their name implies, to reduce the layout of the whole organisation to a piece of paper. Since it shows only the reporting relationships it can be difficult for employees (particularly newcomers) to appreciate the interfacing (formal or informal) they may have with both internal and external 'customers' of their output or 'suppliers' of the input. Relationship charts such as the example which appears over can provide guidance to these relationships and possibly avoid difficulties of a failure to appreciate the need for information, etc. to be passed to another department. The items required by other departments and even the contact could be added to the chart. The circular format lends itself to this type of chart.

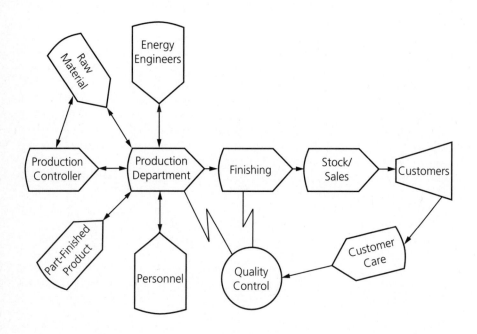

Relationship chart

Such charts are meant to focus on the subject department and show other departments relating to it. Accordingly, each department may need to be provided with such a chart – each appearing in a central position. The subject of these relationships (and the manner in which they should be conducted (i.e. with mutual respect and understanding) should be addressed during any INDUCTION course.

Press releases

Introduction

To much of the media bad news is good news and good news is no news. They know that the attention of their readers is far more likely to be seized and retained if what is featured is a disaster, death or problem (e.g. losing an order leading to redundancies, the failure of a new product or injuries to employees) than if what is featured is the winning of a record order, the development of a new product or the attaining of a safety award. Given this sure way of attracting media attention most organisations will have an understandable aim to avoid such instances. However, disasters do sometimes occur, along with the inevitable media attention. It is thus important that those who report have as many accurate facts about the organisation as possible. As suggested in PUBLIC RELATIONS, however, to ensure accurate reporting of bad news it is important to try to build an ongoing relationship with the media with good news. Whilst this may not command so great attention, properly communicated it may nevertheless capture a few lines in a paper or minutes of air time.

Capturing the attention

Media reporters receive a vast amount of information – much of it unsolicited – and probably use less than 20% of it. There is an obvious need to try to gain for one's piece a uniqueness and an appeal that will make it stand out from the rest. To do this it may help if the factors set out in the following checklist are considered.

Checklist: News release

1. The subject matter must be really newsworthy – not to the organisation but to the readers/listeners/viewers of the media chosen to receive the release.

   Note: *If the item is not newsworthy it is unlikely to be used and the fact that the organisation perceives it to have such value may reflect badly on it – which could in turn adversely affect the next release.*

2. Assuming the subject matter is newsworthy it must be made attention-worthy. Thus the release should both capture initial attention and provide all the relevant information in an easy to read (and easy to use) form.

    Note: *As in most items of written information, if the first paragraph does not grab the reader's attention, no matter how good the rest of the document, it is unlikely to be read. Further, if the release is written in a way whereby the editor can use it (or more likely a part of it) without much editing, rewriting or recourse to the contact named (see below) then it stands a better chance of being used.*

    More fundamentally, editors are busy and under pressure. Anything that makes their job easy is likely to find favour. Conversely anything that makes their job more difficult (e.g. unnecessary, unimportant, verbose releases) will be cast aside. The document will be viewed initially for not much more than 10 seconds – if it hasn't indicated it is going to make the editor's life easier in those 10 seconds its destination will be the bin.

3. The release should be as brief as possible commensurate with the subject matter. Further, the language used should be simple, straightforward and should avoid jargon. Trying to 'pad out' a short release with extraneous information is more likely to mean the whole thing is cast aside.

    Note: *If an editor starts to puzzle over wording and descriptions they will know that many of their readers will similarly puzzle – except that they won't puzzle for long before passing on to the next item. A paper or programme full of such items will soon lose appeal so it is not in their interests to feature such items. Similarly they are human and it may be easier to use a short item than a long one which will require considerable work on their part to edit and pare it to the essentials.*

4. A release is not the place to build to a climax. The most important point should be featured first or prominently. Everything else should support or explain this 'headline' material.

    Note: *This re-emphasises the need to project the most important point in the most important place – the first paragraph. Even titles or headlines may be able to capture the attention:*

    £5 million lottery win, 20 new Bloggs jobs

    is likely to capture the attention in a way that

> **Bloggs is proud to announce that it has been successful in acquiring a grant of £5,075,014 from the Foundation responsible for distributing money generated by the National Lottery which will result in the company employing an additional 20 part-time staff over the next nine months**

never can.

5. A release is not the correct conduit for organisation promotion. Obviously every piece of good news about the organisation may help promote it, but the purpose of a release is to provide information that it is believed will be of interest to the readers/listeners/viewers as a news item – not as promotional puff. The editor perceiving that the purpose of the release is purely to act as a promotion for the organisation may well bin it rather than be manipulated in this way by its author.

6. A pithy quotation from the Managing Director, or better still from a household-name customer (or equivalent), breathes life into the report. Readers tend to repeat quotations in their head as if someone was speaking to them, and thus may give greater attention to the quote than to the copy – this is particularly true if the voice is known, since they can replay the words in their head as if the person was saying them.

7. If the release features a product, and it is feasible to do so, include a sample with it. As a (poor) substitute, a photograph might be used but it will carry far less weight. If a number of photographs are available, reference to this in the release and a crib of what is available might generate interest, providing obtaining the photo is made easy and in a form capable of being used by the editor.

> *Note:* *If samples are sent, the greatest care should be taken to send the best-quality items. There are cases on record where, far from generating a nice little 'plug' for the product, the item was castigated, as was the organisation by association, because of a faulty sample.*
>
> *Anything that implies difficulty will deter interest. Stating 'details of a range of photos are available from the Public Relations office' is unlikely to spark a request – the editor has no synopsis of what is available, no personal contact or time giving guidance to making the request. There isn't even a telephone number, although it is assumed one is on the release somewhere – but is it the same office? 'Too difficult – don't bother' may be the instinctive reaction.*

8. Where the release provides advance information about a forthcoming event ensure that the information is 'advance'. Giving less than a

week's notification is unlikely to generate an interest. Similarly, more than a month may result in the item being overlooked, although a reminder (possibly by phone or e-mail) can be effective.

9. Keep a careful note of the correct names, positions and addresses of all those on the mailing lists – and keep all the details up-to-date. Addressing releases to the wrong person, or the right person with the wrong title (or either at the wrong address) reflects poorly on the organisation, and with an adversely written or spoken news item there is a temptation to pull in the badly addressed item as a further indication of the type of organisation it is.

10. Always give a contact name and telephone number, *and* ensure that the contact is available on that number for some days after the release has been issued. If this is impossible then stating certain times when the person will be there is helpful, but may reduce the likelihood of contact being attempted.

> *Note:* *Contact names may be given because it is felt the release does not (or cannot) provide comprehensive information in a sufficiently clear exposition. If this is so it might be better to rewrite the release, as it should be capable of standing on its own. The contact name should be there only in case the editor wishes to feature more information or obtain supporting data.*

Golden rules – the four ONLYS

1. Issue a release ONLY when something of interest to the target audience is to be featured.
2. Issue a release ONLY if it passes the 'blind man's test'.
    (Read the release once only (since it will be read aloud this may itself suggest improvement to the author) to someone who knows nothing of the subject matter and will have no chance to re-read it. Ask them to state the story. Unless they can repeat the salient facts the release needs to be rewritten – and probably shortened.)
3. Issue a release ONLY to the particular sections of the media likely to be interested in the item. Few national papers are likely to be interested in the fact that the public relations manager has been appointed to the Board. However, if the manager is a member of the Institute of Public Relations, no doubt the editor of their journal might wish to feature it. The temptation 'Oh let's send it to everyone anyway' should be resisted since when there is something of interest it may be treated (i.e. spiked unused) in the same way as the promotion of the PR manager (deserved though it may be!).
4. Issue a release ONLY if there is someone always on call ready and prepared to answer questions and provide additional data should the target media channel require this.

Public relations

Introduction

The operations and activities of organisations (particularly those that are in any way viewed as 'suspect' or 'questionable') are increasingly subject to the attention of 'the media' and/or the public, either as stories in their own right, or as part of a larger, and possibly investigative, 'story'. Even the manner in which employees are treated can now be scrutinised and commented upon as a result of media attention to Industrial Tribunal hearings of what would once have been regarded as internal matters. Inevitably, the incidence of such attention is greater for those organisations which are 'household names'.

Since attention can arise and/or increase dramatically when a crisis in the operation occurs, all organisations should, at least, consider the need for media and public interfacing.

Whether the responsibility for public relations is recognised or not it occurs every day. Each time a customer buys a product or service a 'public relationship' occurs. Indeed, nowhere is dealing with PR positively and constructively more vital than in handling customers, and particularly their complaints. Despite this being completely obvious, surprisingly few organisations think of linking, however tenuously, the activities of the CUSTOMER CARE and public relations departments and perhaps the most pertinent piece of advice in considering public relations as a discipline would be to make it responsible for dealing with customers – particularly their problems.

Reputation

The reputation of a company, and public awareness of it, may be indefinable and incapable of quantification, nevertheless it is very important. A reputation can take years to build – and just seconds to lose – as witness the events following Gerald Ratner's presentation to the Institute of Directors, (recounted in CORPORATE STYLE). This is a particularly apposite example of how thoughtless words can wreck a reputation, with the added irony that the crisis was generated internally. Most crises develop externally and when they do combine to challenge its reputation or survival, the organisation that is unprepared for this, that has not cultivated media connections or has not rehearsed for the investigative or even hostile approach, or the disaster (see CRISIS COMMUNICATION) may find it virtually impossible to counter adverse comment, or to put over its own case. A comprehensive approach incorporating policy, research, crisis-reaction, training and practice is essential.

Policy

A suitable policy/procedure of which the following is a draft could be adopted:

Checklist: Public relations commitment

1. The organisation recognises the natural interest that will be evinced by the media on behalf of the public and the public itself in its operations and will make all information, other than that which is regarded as confidential, regularly available primarily to accredited sources.

    Note: Such sources could include named journalists, a list of journals, newsletters, radio and TV outlets (as well as any WEB SITE), etc., who would automatically be sent all literature produced for external use.

2. [Name and deputy] will act as spokesperson for the organisation and will be briefed continually by [directors/executives as applicable] those responsible for each [division, product, etc.]
3. In the event of other employees being contacted by representatives of the media, they will refer them to the spokesperson.
4. In interfacing with the media, the spokesperson will endeavour to be truthful at all times, and to ensure that information is correctly reported.
5. Contacts will be made with each branch of the media regularly briefed, so that they have background knowledge of the organisation, which is fully up-to-date.
6. In the event of a serious occurrence the senior manager responsible must brief the spokesperson as quickly as possible.
7. On no occasion, regardless of the circumstances, should the products, services or reputation of the organisation or of any person working in it or of any third party connected with it be called into doubt or question in any way whatever without the knowledge of [name].

Research

The above policy statement covers the whole area of media/public interest in very general terms. As far as the spokesperson is concerned, however, s/he will need to have access to a range of data and to be in command of the latest developments. No media briefing or interview will be successful unless adequate preparation and research has been carried out. Thus the following are necessary:

1. Identify the areas of operation in which the media/public could be interested.
2. Identify the target audiences and the information they will require.
3. Identify the nature of the interest of each part of the target audience and what information will be required.
4. Establish who is to deal with the ongoing enquiry and how they are to be briefed and updated concerning progress and all related aspects.
5. Encourage the spokesperson to create links with representatives of all media (establishing names, positions, main interests or 'angles', deadlines, potential bias, etc.).
6. Regularly examine stories and reports concerning the organisation to ensure the (correct/ required/positive) image is being created.
7. Continually develop questions (and, more importantly, answers thereto) that the organisation least wants asked and become conversant with both (updated as necessary).
8. Prepare and update a résumé of all the successes of the organisation so that good news is available which may leaven the bad.

Example: Controlling bad news

The difficulty many organisations experience is that often the media are only interested when there is bad news mainly since they know, human nature being what it is, many people are likely to pay more attention to or be more attracted by 'bad news' than good. During an interview concerned with bad news, particularly if it reflects poorly on the organisation, some rapport with or positive feeling from the audience may be gained if the spokesperson can introduce details of facts that show the organisation in a better light. This needs to be done with care and in appreciation of the subject matter of the enquiry. Introducing details of record production last week when the subject is the death of an employee would be crass and unfeeling, and would generate entirely the wrong impression. However, mentioning that in 50 years of production on the site and in a workforce of 20,000 personnel, this incident, whilst being extremely sad, is the first fatality, could at least, though not detracting from the tragic current circumstances, place the incident in some kind of perspective. Being able to state that the organisation is caring for relatives and has called an independent third party to investigate the circumstances thoroughly might also help. 'No comment' is not an option if some respect for the organisation is to be preserved.

Crisis reaction

Whilst briefing the media on the more mundane aspects of organisation performance may be relatively easy, dealing with such interest in the aftermath of a calamity or disaster, poses considerable problems capable of being tackled only if based on contingency planning, i.e. anticipating the disaster and making advance plans for dealing with the effects (see CRISIS COMMUNICATION). The advantage of 'planning for disaster' is that lengthy and calm thought can be given to alternative tactics and reactions, without the considerable time pressure for reaction that the incidence of disaster can cause. In addition, consideration of alternative actions in the event of disaster, may suggest beneficial changes in current operations. Obviously, if it is to be of value such planning must be both comprehensive and regularly updated. Accordingly it will be an expensive operation, albeit one that should be regarded as an investment – certainly trying to cope with the innumerable requirements for action and comments following a disaster without at least a little planning will be virtually impossible.

Checklist: Crisis reaction – communication aspects

1. Initial contact will usually be by telephone. A person should be nominated (possibly the Company Secretary, though there should always be one or two back-up personnel) to handle all initial queries if the spokesperson is not available.
2. Listen carefully to what the enquirer is asking.
3. Make notes of (or tape) the call content, time, the caller's name, position and media represented, the caller's telephone number and location.
4. *Do not* respond to questions, comments, observations – simply make notes as set out in 3 above, and state that by a (given) time someone will respond either in a news release or by telephone, e-mail, etc.
5. *Do not* be flustered by indications of deadlines. Those are the caller's problems, not yours. Attempted insistence on immediate response, outrageous accusations, innuendoes, etc., should also be noted but not commented upon.

6. By the time promised (not less than an hour) ensure someone does ring the caller back with comments.
7. Keep responses, press statements, etc., short. Verbal embroidery can both offset the punch effect and provide angles from which the reporter can come back at the author.
8. Provide a contact name/number.
9. Should such contact be used, the above guidelines should be applied – if necessary with the spokesperson ringing back after time for thought.

Interviews

The spokesperson needs considerable personal knowledge of the organisation which can be augmented by detailed input from time to time by those personally responsible. However, such background whilst essential is not sufficient. Excellent chairmen (the normal spokespeople for corporate matters) do not necessarily make excellent spokesmen when other issues are under review, and training for such circumstances is essential. The person must be able to keep calm under pressure, to think swiftly, to appreciate that some answers may be double-edged (i.e. that either of two responses may be self-critical) and to try to avoid this effect, and to show their knowledge is sound. The items in the following checklist should be addressed:

Checklist: Spokesperson interview briefing

1. Before agreeing to the interview discover as much as possible about the circumstances (name of interviewer, programme, general purpose, scope of enquiry, whether live or recorded, scope for restricting/controlling questions, length of item to be used and likely release date, etc.)
2. Prepare as comprehensive and complete brief as possible on the subject matter and supporting items – organisation data, performance, products, problems, plans, etc.
3. If the topic is likely to be controversial or embarrassing to the person or organisation appropriate responses and statements should be prepared, ideally trying to limit the 'damage' that could be caused or to develop news which mitigates the effect.
4. The spokesperson needs to have total control of the brief, of all facts and of prepared responses, to be able to speak knowledgeably concerning the subject matter. Any hesitation, lack of confidence or inadequate knowledge will be communicated to the listener or viewer

and create doubt and/or undermine veracity. In this respect it may be better to admit 'I don't know' rather than trying to 'flannel' through an answer. At least saying 'I don't know' (although it should only be used once or twice in any one interview) does have the ring of truth about it and can indicate – and win plaudits for – honesty and straightforwardness. (See the case study concerning Chrysler in CRISIS COMMUNICATION.)

5. Three or four simple messages, or arguments that the organisation wishes to promote, must be developed, possibly with 'changes of direction' sentences, so that if the interviewer leads off in one direction, the spokesperson may be able to direct it to the organisation's preferred message. This approach needs to be controlled since a constant refusal to answer the actual questions put may lead to a more inquisitive or confrontational interview.

6. There should be no assumption that the interviewer will not have full knowledge of all the facts. It is better to assume that everything is known and then prepare answers accordingly.

7. The spokesperson must be ready for the 'off the cuff' and unrehearsed question deliberately introduced and designed to catch him/her unawares, leading to the making of an unprepared or unwise comment or answer.

8. Above all the spokesperson must be able to keep calm under pressure and/or goading, to be able to think quickly and laterally in order to fend off aggression and criticism, to retain control, and **never** to lose their temper.

Case study: Lose your temper – lose the argument

During one of the periodical examinations of top people's pay the chairman of one of the privatised utilities was being interviewed on television. His salary had recently increased substantially and the interviewer wanted to know why. Instead of explaining the impact of market forces on salaries, the increased productivity, and other quantifiable achievements, the chairman lost his temper on camera. The sight was unedifying and displayed a lack of preparedness for the questions which reflected badly not only on the chairman but also on his staff who should have briefed him.

---

9. The spokesperson must recognise that most live media interviews last a minute or less and thus it may be possible only to put across two or three authoritative comments. They need to be calm, alert and

interested and serious – a spokesperson should never try to be humorous, flustered or flippant. To a large extent, particularly on television, the manner in which a message is delivered can be more important than its content.

10. The spokesperson should take a reasonable length of time to think about the questions – asking for them to be repeated if necessary.

11. False statements should not be allowed to pass unchecked – the record should be corrected, tactfully but firmly.

12. Be positive not defensive. It may be better to 'own up' to a bad performance or event with a 'promise to improve' or rectify, rather than trying to defend an untenable position. The latter alternative will normally display the organisation in a poor light regardless of the circumstances – the impression will be 'they have learned nothing from the mistake', so nothing will change. This is particularly important when there has been serious loss, injury or death. In such instances it is essential that genuine sympathy is expressed and that there is an indication that steps are being taken to try to ensure there is no repetition.

Instant reactions

There is an increasing tendency to try to obtain at least a few sentences of comment from spokespersons as they leave (for example a meeting or building). Since this practice is widespread it should not take people by surprise, yet there are instances when even those experienced in answering intrusive questions 'lose their cool'. The solution is to expect that there will be such questions and rather than exiting immediately take some minutes to consider the worst questions and suitable answers, bearing in mind that although 'no comment' may not be the best answer in such circumstances, at least it will be preferable to losing one's temper. In visual terms someone saying nothing cannot be tolerated – the producer will quickly cut the sequence.

Case study: Lose your temper lose the argument

A former head of a stock exchange in the Far East was subjected to intrusive questioning at a press conference which was being televised live. He took such exception to some of the questions that he attempted to lean across the desk and hit the reporter. He was later imprisoned for several malpractices but even had this not occurred it would have been difficult for him to have resumed his position after such a public exhibition.

Suggestion schemes

Introduction

Any process whereby management and employees enjoy a dialogue is a means of communication. In many organisations the success of suggestion schemes is generally measured in financial terms – useful suggestions generally pay for themselves many times over. However, there are three other aspects of value in such schemes which are often overlooked:

1. The fact that employees are considering and discussing ideas for improvement of products, practices and procedures displays considerable commitment from the employees to their employer which can only be beneficial. For every suggestion committed to paper and submitted via the scheme there are doubtless a further five ideas which were made in passing and implemented without further ado and with little recognition.

2. Employees are engaged in a process of communication which even if it does not immediately lead to a valuable idea should at least mean that motivation and commitment are enhanced.

3. If employee suggestions have been implemented then those employees responsible will be committed to making the ideas work. This is bound to have a beneficial effect both in terms of productivity and loyalty to the company.

Purpose

Obviously the main purpose of the scheme should be to reward employees for making suggestions which occur to them for improving output, reducing costs and/or waste, improving efficiency, developing new products, etc. However, an equally important aspect of the scheme is that it creates an environment which encourages thought and suggestions regarding the ways in which the status quo can be improved. The introduction of such a scheme needs careful planning, whilst its operation needs constant promotion and support.

Checklist: Suggestion scheme implementation

1. Plan the whole scheme carefully – ensuring that as many employees as possible are eligible. Almost inevitably it will be necessary to exclude those involved in research and development (part of whose responsibilities will normally include generating new ideas) as well as those involved in production study, organisation and methods, and anyone else with similar duties.

2. Appoint a senior manager to take responsibility for introducing and running the scheme. With a large workforce the time requirements should not be underestimated. The fact that a senior person is involved will also indicate that top management is committed to the concept.

3. Set up a judging panel which should be (and be seen to be) objective and impartial. Representatives of employees should sit on such a panel, (perhaps a non-executive director or someone not directly connected with the organisation). To avoid accusations of unfairness, etc., no one connected with the judging panel should be able to make a suggestion and benefit from the scheme.

4. Rewards should be paid for valuable ideas. The going rate seems to be about a fifth of the value of the idea. It may be helpful for each idea adopted to calculate its useful life (restricted to a period no longer than, say, three years) and pay out a proportion of the value each year.

5. The paperwork should be kept as simple as possible. Whilst it is tempting to require all suggestions to be made on similar forms this may restrict some employees' contributions; and thus the suggestion that is scribbled on the legendary 'back of an envelope' should not be ruled out.

6. Confidentiality should be preserved to minimise the possibility of 'poaching' of ideas. This can be achieved by the suggestions being handed in sealed envelopes to the administrator and a receipt bearing a rough guide to the idea being given to the 'suggester'. This should bear the date that the idea was presented.

7. All ideas should be given an initial consideration and a likely decision (that is acceptance or not) within two weeks of submission.

8. The scheme should be given constant and original publicity. Whenever an award is made, photos should be taken and promoted widely.

9. The success of the scheme depends on the commitment of the workforce to the concept. As such, rather like the idea of the house journal or newspaper, the whole scheme must have an element of fun, or at least of being enjoyable.

10. As well as individual awards it may be helpful to award an additional 'star-prize' to the most valuable suggestion in a year. If the value of individual suggestions is not thought likely to amount to a great deal, it

may be advisable to make this subject either to the total exceeding a set figure or to an individual suggestion exceeding that figure.

Promotion

An essential aspect of all such schemes is the need to keep promoting it and to keep management and employee interest alive and active in its support. To this end regular updates of progress on suggestions that have been implemented should be provided. It may also help if awards are made annually – for example, where a suggestion has a life of three years, the award in respect of each year's savings or additional earnings could be made in each year. If the awards are made at a well-publicised function this will also help keep interest in the scheme alive. The use of a star-prize award for the best suggestion received each year may also aid in this respect.

Case study: Richer by far

Richer Sounds is a 70-employee, £12-million-turnover company that readily acknowledges that it receives many of its best ideas from its staff. Examples include a discount scheme which boosted sales tenfold, and a policy of telephoning customers to check that they were happy with a repair service. The company funds monthly brainstorming sessions for employees in pubs local to the company's 12 stores. The number of suggestions made by each store count towards a competition won by the store with most suggestions. All suggestions whether accepted or not are rewarded by the company. The rewards range from £5 to a trip on the *Orient Express.*

> **Key technique**
>
> The employer is using the scheme not just to generate ideas to help improve profits, but also as a social event and a means of generating some competitive spirit, both of which help to bind individuals into teams and the company together.

(from David Martin, *How to Control your Costs and Increase your Profits* Director Books, 1992.)

Case study: Inflating the profits

An employee at Dunlop General Rubber Products in Manchester suggested, via the company's 'Bright Spark' suggestion scheme, a change to the way the company cut the foam rubber used in vehicle mats. The suggestion reduced waste and saved the company £7,500 a year. Another employee suggested a new method of removing the blemishes from rubber products which saved the company over £12,000, part of the £54,000 saved in one year alone by the company from ideas generated by its own scheme.

Key technique

The value of these two suggestions may be somewhat larger than the average, but all, large or small, add to the profits. Dunlop gives a corporate pen to every contributor as well as a mug bearing the slogan 'I am a Dunlop Bright Spark' to those whose ideas are taken up; this not only recognises the employee's input but also acts as a reminder to make more suggestions.

Summary financial statements

Content

An SFS must be consistent with the full accounts and the auditors are required to certify that this is so. The SFS must state whether the auditors' report on the full accounts was qualified or not. It is also required by law to contain the items set out in the following checklist.

Checklist: Content of SFS

1. *Key section of the directors' report*

    - business review
    - post balance-sheet events
    - future developments
    - directors' details

2. *A summary profit and loss account containing*

- pre-tax profit/loss for financial period
- tax and post-tax profit
- extraordinary and exceptional items
- dividends paid and proposed
- directors' payments

3. *A summary balance sheet including*

- issued share capital
- reserves
- provisions
- liabilities and assets
- contingent liabilities

4. *An auditors' report*

General requirements

(a) In producing an SFS the time limits for production and filing of the accounts as set out in Section 244 of the Companies Act (1985) must not have expired.

(b) The SFS must be approved by the Board, and ultimately by the shareholders, and an original must be signed by a director (whose name must appear on each copy).

(c) The document must state that members have a right to the full set of accounts and be accompanied by a printed, pre-paid card requesting that the shareholders be sent the full accounts.

(d) If the auditors' report on the full report is in any way qualified then a copy of the full report must accompany the SFS.

(e) The SFS itself must give sufficient information to be useful and representative.

Options

To discover whether shareholders would prefer to have the SFS, companies must first either

- send both summary statement and full report to their shareholders with a reply paid card, stating that unless the shareholder indicates, he will in future only be sent the summary version, or
- canvas their shareholders in advance to discover who wishes to receive the summary version.

Execution

Since the aim is to produce a simplified report, the precepts of presentation set out in the sections on EMPLOYEE REPORTS, GRAPHICS and JARGON, need to be considered. Obviously in considering the preparation of such a report it must be borne in mind that although there may be savings in production and postage of the full report, there will be additional costs (not least in time of the compiler) in originating a further report. If the organisation produces or needs an EMPLOYEE REPORT, it may actually be cost-effective to produce and send such a document to the shareholders, since experience indicates that most shareholders like and do read such documents, even though they may not read the annual report.

Effectiveness

Although there seems little doubt that it is possible for companies with large numbers of private shareholders to save considerable sums if those shareholders or a large proportion opt to receive only an SFS, the document has received relatively little recognition, and indeed where the company already prepared an EMPLOYEE REPORT and sent that to the shareholders as well as the annual report it seems there was a higher acceptance of that report than the legally recognised SFS. Research summarised in a report, *Summary Financial Statements – the way forward* (July 1996, Institute of Chartered Accountants in England and Wales), indicated that fewer than 40 companies had opted to produce an SFS, although where one was available there was a high take up from private shareholders (over 90% in most cases). The fact that relatively few companies have produced such a document is surprising given that

- the research indicated that 'the full Report and Accounts has become so complicated that most private shareholders simply lose the plot' and
- the 'most eloquent endorsement of SFS is the undeniable fact that shareholders actually like them'.

As one of the contributors to the report (Smith & Nephew Plc) commented, 'We remained with the SFS approach because we believe that the complexity of modern accounting disclosures militates against clarity of communication'.

Postscript: Sadly some SFS now run to 40 pages or more which rather negates their whole purpose.

VIPs

Introduction

The addition of a known 'name' to an organisation's event (e.g. the launch of a new product) may seem to be one way of ensuring that the event gains media coverage and the organisation gains prestige. Whilst this may be so, it can add a considerable dimension to the items that will need to be addressed by the event organiser, even if the VIP is a personal contact of someone in the organisation.

Contact

Most VIPs in the entertainment and sporting fields have managers or agents through whom arrangements can be made. This may be simpler than making arrangements direct, as those involved will usually have some experience of the requirements and may be able to offer advice on a range of subjects – not least the fee to be charged. Other than personal contacts, few VIPs will be prepared to 'sing for their supper' without some recompense, even if rather than being paid personally, they require a donation to be made to a charity. The other advantage of dealing with an agent is that if, having set a budget for the event, the fee proposed for the required VIP is too high, alternatives may be available.

When agreeing a fee either direct with the VIP or with an agent it is necessary to set out clearly exactly what is covered by the fee. The organisation needs to know:

- the basic fee
- whether travel expenses are additional and if so at what rate they are charged and (if a mileage charge) what distance is required to be covered
- whether there are any other expenses to be met for the VIP and/or for any staff accompanying them (e.g. dinner/accommodation for chauffeur, PA, etc.)
- whether there is a booking fee payable to an agent or manager
- whether any insurance cover is required to be taken out, and so on.

All such items should be confirmed in writing – a confirmation which might prudently contain a statement that the content reflects the full exposure of the organisation in respect of the booking of the VIP. The question of cancellation (of either side), and the financial effects of this, should also be addressed.

If the VIP is well known then early booking will be required as the diaries of such people tend to be booked many months – even years – ahead.

Special arrangements

The following checklist provides guidance to a number of matters that need attention, but should not be taken as exhaustive.

1. If the VIP is to be fed and/or accommodated any dietary or special accommodation requests need to be known and then checked for availability.
2. If a speech is to be delivered, who is to prepare this? If it is the VIP personally, do they need details of the organisation, etc., so that they can add 'local colour' to what they have to say?
3. Does the VIP require the organisation to provide transport? If so, the preferred type of transport (as well as times and locations) needs to be agreed and arranged.
4. Any requirements as to dress which are placed on the guests need to be communicated to the VIP for guidance as to their appearance.
5. The purpose and subject matter of the event will need to be clearly defined and a note given to the VIP.

Case study: Inappropriate

A famous comedian was booked as an after-dinner speaker at an old boys' reunion dinner-dance. However, although details of the college were passed to the comedian's manager no one thought to mention that the college was run by an order of religious brothers. The comedian's speech contained a number of risqué and even blue jokes which were not appreciated by all the audience, many of whom were embarrassed not so much for themselves as for the representatives of the religious order present.

---

6. If the purpose is to deliver a speech, the VIP may wish to leave immediately afterwards. If so, transport at the required time should be made available. If the VIP does not intend leaving, then a minder needs to be nominated to look after the guest until they do leave. This may

involve additional expense since it is not unknown for some VIPs to remain for the whole event (some even drinking heavily).

7. Will a changing (or resting) room be required where the VIP can relax until required? If so any preferences as to type of room, refreshments, etc., need to be addressed.

8. Is anything known of the VIP's behaviour at such functions? Ideally enquiry should be made to try to discover where the VIP has 'performed' before, and contact should be made with the organiser to check whether there were any idiosyncrasies or eccentricities for which the organiser needs to be prepared (e.g. excess capacity for alcohol, etc.)

9. If the media is to cover the event, the VIP needs to be told, and any reactions dealt with. Few will object to being featured, but may insist that their own press release including personal details, plans, etc., be given to the media. Arrangements need to be made to deliver this data.

10. If the VIP is required to speak they should be briefed on whether the event is to be attended by media in case believing themseves to be in a private function, they are perhaps less discreet than they should be.

11. The question of guests (and others) taking photographs needs to be addressed. Most VIPs will not be bothered but some may object (some have even tried to charge) and it would be wise to be aware of this before the event and to advise guests and others accordingly.

12. Similarly the VIP's preferences regarding questions, autographs, etc., need to be checked and those involved advised.

13. Some VIPs need special security arrangements which may cause considerable disruption to the location of the event. This will need to be agreed with the person in charge of the location – whether internal or external.

Case study: Security alert

It is not only at special functions that security needs to be checked. When Margaret Thatcher was Prime Minister, her husband was a director of a number of companies. When he attended Board meetings at the premises of those companies they were subject to a police search for fear of terrorist devices.

---

14. Any external location should be advised that the VIP is to attend and requested to assist in making their presence welcome. It may even be possible to obtain some financial and/or other concession(s) from an external location which perceives it could benefit from the publicity that may accompany the attendance of the VIP.

Note: *Echoing the above case study, some VIPs make prefer to keep their visits confidential until the last minute.*

General

As in most other aspects of communication where there is a high profile it is essential to prepare and to note down all items with an allocation of responsibilities. Ideally (particularly for example if the VIP is to perform an opening of a building) one or more rehearsals might be advisable. If it is impossible for the VIP to attend it may be possible to video the rehearsal with someone standing in for the VIP, and to give this to them in advance so that they can see what they are expected to do. In addition a comprehensive 'script' giving all directions should be prepared. Once a dummy-run, following exactly what the script says (to check it is accurate) has been carried out, the script can be given to the VIP, whilst someone should be nominated to act as their personal 'prompt' during the execution of the required activity.

Royal visitors

It might be thought that in the event of a royal visitor being the VIP the amount of work would increase considerably, not least because of the additional security and protocol that must be observed. In fact this is not necessarily so, since royal households have people whose sole function it is to ensure that such visits run smoothly; thus the company's role is more likely to be one of accepting instructions, rather than being proactive in making arrangements.

Web site and the internet

Introduction

The development of the internet (which originated in the USA when several educational and research institutions decided to link their computers to share access to their research material – a development which was quickly copied by the American military) has been rapid and all-embracing. In less than a decade the internet has gone from a science-fiction dream to a multi-billion-pound industry, with around 100 million subscribers to the world-wide web in 152 countries. The web is seeing its traffic increase at a phenomenal rate – it increased tenfold in 1994 alone and 10% of the total use emanates from the UK. So rapid has been the take up of the system that reporters are suggesting that unless a business is linked to the internet within the next few years they will not be in business within a further 20 years, not least since it has been estimated that by 2000 commercial transactions using the internet could exceed ECU 200 billion – a massive transfer of trade from traditional means. The effect of this, and the consequent rise in teleworking (the Henley Centre estimated in 1995 that there could be 10 million teleworkers in the UK by the year 2010), could cause massive changes in the lives of those in the developed world.

Creating a web page

In terms of communication the web offers organisations the chance to inform all the millions of subscribers world-wide of a considerable range of information on themselves, their products, services, etc. It thus provides a relatively cheap means of promoting the entity and its products and, with an interactive site, of actually taking orders and generating custom. However, the question of the laws governing such transactions need to be considered and to restrict potential liability organisations may need to specify and restrict those with whom they are prepared to trade and to endeavour to stipulate that its terms are an integral part of the contract before a contract is actually completed. In addition it may need to be made clear that the information at a web site provides an 'invitation to treat' (rather as shops display goods in their windows at certain prices) rather than a commitment to supply, in order to avoid the difficulties that may arise should the organisation be unable to meet the demand generated.

Interactive pages apart, in many respects a basic web page, despite the technology, resembles the humblest paper memo: it cannot communicate. Its value lies in being able to provide information on a variety of topics including products, with the advantage that, being held electronically, the number of words used is infinite (a great advantage over the memo). The danger is that such information needs to be constantly updated and failure to do so can lead the organisation into legal difficulties.

Case study: Caught out

A leading transatlantic airline displayed details of its fares, including special deals and discounts on its web site in the USA. Having checked the web site for details, a traveller tried to book a seat on the discount basis shown on the web page. Unfortunately the time limit to take advantage of the discount had expired but no one had either inserted a cut-off date in the web information or changed the data when the offer duration expired. The company was fined $14,000 for displaying misleading information.

Key technique

Since the difference in price of the discounted and full price ticket was apparently only $19, one would have thought that someone in the company should have had the sense to recognise the mistake and honour the traveller's request.

Note: *The possibility of creating a libel, or grounds for libel, is detailed in ELECTRONIC TRANSMISSIONS. Since nearly 90% of the web's transmissions are for the purpose of sending e-mails it follows that much of its traffic is party-specific, some of which will be confidential to those parties. However, the risk of others being able to see confidential information is high.*

Demand

Dangers apart, the demand for a site is growing. A 1996 survey by leading PR consultants, Manning Selvage and Leed, reports that '74% of companies already have a web site or are planning one', mainly for PR purposes. Further such sites will be interactive – a feature expected to grow phenomenally by the year 2000.

The advantage of a web site over traditional methods of providing information to the target audience (press, mailing, etc.) is that it can always be up-to-date. In theory an operator could be retained to update it as every single item changes – minute by minute. This level of updating is perhaps unnecessary, but daily updating is entirely practical.

What is essential is that those who wish (or may wish) to use a web site should register their proposed name through Nominet UK which since 1996 has been performing the equivalent job for web names that the Registrar of Companies does for company names. There have already been problems for leading companies caused by others registering their names for web sites. Even British Telecommunications found the name 'British Telecom' had been registered by a private individual and had to initiate legal proceedings to recover its 'property'.

Danger

It is estimated that one computer linked to the internet is hacked into every 20 seconds. Before you leave a beach to go surfing ensure your most valuable asset (i.e. the information in the computer you are using) is safely protected – alternatively use one computer with no files in its memory to surf, and another not connected to the internet, to work.

> *Note:* *The implication of the European Union's Distance Selling Directive, expected to become effective fairly shortly should be considered in this regard, whilst the European Commission has already published a guidance paper 'Initiative on Electronic Commerce' setting out its objectives in terms of electronic trading.*

Zygote

A zygote is a cell. It is formed and can only be formed by the joining of two gametes. Once formed the cell can grow. Left separate and alone neither of the gametes can grow.

Information is a one-way process. Communication is a two-way process dependent on feedback. The interaction of two parties is required before there can be any communication. Only if there is communication can the parties grow in understanding of one another.

The solutions to organisational problems frequently lie not in the executive suite but in the collective intelligence of the workforce.

(Peter Drucker)

With the best will in the world and the best Board in the world and the best strategic direction in the world, nothing will happen unless everyone down the line understands what they are trying to achieve and gives of their best.

(Sir John Harvey Jones)

If this world of ours is to succeed we must teach the art of understanding each other at really practical levels.

(Mountbatten of Burma)

How can we begin to understand unless we first communicate?